# TRADE SMART

## SOMRAJ DUTTA

(CWM. MBA. CTA. B.SC.. SEBI REGD. RIA)

Imprint and Copyright



First Edition, 2024

The material in this book also appears in the print version of this title:



Capital Media Products (including Books like this) are available at special quantity discounts to use as premiums and sales promotions, or for use in corporate training programs. For more information, please contact Dutt, Special Sales, at connectdutt@gmail.com or (91) 033-2415-3303 (India).

Acknowledgment

From a longstanding curiosity about Wall Street to the serendipity of landing my initial professional role in the financial services sector in India, my journey over the past two decades has been a captivating ride. Throughout this period, I immersed myself in understanding the intricacies of the Retail Banking, with invaluable guidance from influential figures such as Mr. S Krishnan, Ms. Jayati Chakraborty and Mr. Aditya Mandloi, who significantly contributed to my corporate education. Meanwhile, I developed an insatiable curiosity to master the Capital Markets. Concurrently, one of my aunts played a pivotal role, consistently fostering my enthusiasm for investing from a very early age.

Reflecting on my time at Standard Chartered Bank, CITI and HSBC evoke a sense of nostalgia. The 20+ years spent with these behemoths (so to speak), collaborating with industry leaders, eclipsed the educational impact of my tenure at the Indian Institute of Management, Lucknow. Although my academic focus was on Corporate Strategy, it uniquely steered me towards my current exploration of companies and their role in shaping the market.

# Disclaimer

Every effort has been made to make this book as accurate as possible. The purpose of this book is to educate. In case of any review of evidence that is presented for informational purposes. No individual should use the information in this book as Financial Advice. Any application of the advice herein is at the reader's own discretion and risk. Therefore any individual who has a specific financial problem should seek the counsel of a Registered Financial Advisor before he/ she implements any advice in this book.

The author and Capital Media Publishers, shall have neither liability nor responsibility to any person or entity with respect to loss, damage, or injury caused or alleged to be caused directly or indirectly by the information contained in this book. We assume no responsibility for errors, inaccuracies, omissions, or any inconsistency herein. Any slights of people, places, or organizations are unintentional.

# About the Author

Somraj Dutta, a Chartered Wealth Manager (CWM) and MBA graduate with distinction from United Business Institutes, Belgium, brings over 12 years of expertise as a Professional Investor and Trader with the National Stock Exchange, India.

As a Vice President with HSBC, with additional experience in CITI Bank and Standard Chartered Bank, he boasts 20+ years in Retail Banking and Financial Services.

Holding a Certified Technical Trading (CTA) Professional title from the National Stock Exchange, Somraj is also a Securities & Exchanges Board of India (SEBI), Registered Financial Planner and consultant, offering advisory to his clients.

His multifaceted career includes journalism, authorship, and over 6 years of Corporate and Financial Training with renowned entities such as Sharekhan and American Academy of Financial Management.

As a life member of All India Management Association and a Fellow of the American Academy of Financial Management, USA, Somraj is now an accomplished educator, author, consultant, and speaker trainer, bringing a holistic approach to wealth management.

# Dedication

At The Blessed Feet of The Lord

# Acknowledgment

From a longstanding curiosity about Wall Street to the serendipity of landing my initial professional role in the financial services sector in India, my journey over the past two decades has been a captivating ride. Throughout this period, I immersed myself in understanding the intricacies of the Retail Banking, with invaluable guidance from influential figures such as Mr. S Krishnan, Ms. Jayati Chakraborty and Mr. Aditya Mandloi, who significantly contributed to my corporate education. Meanwhile I developed an insatiable curiosity to master the Capital Markets. Concurrently, one of my aunts played a pivotal role, consistently fostering my enthusiasm for investing from a very early age.

Reflecting on my time at Standard Chartered Bank, CITI and HSBC evokes a sense of nostalgia. The 20+ years spent with these behemoths (so to speak), collaborating with industry leaders, eclipsed the educational impact of my tenure at the Indian Institute of Management, Lucknow. Although my academic focus was on Corporate Strategy, it uniquely steered me towards my current exploration of companies and their role in shaping the market.

# Quote

"I'm always thinking about losing money as opposed to making money. Don't focus on making money, focus on protecting what you have."

— Paul Tudor Jones

# Foreword

Embarking on a journey in the world of investing and trading over the past 12 years has been a profound learning experience for me. When I first started trading, I had no real plan at all. My only "strategy," if I can call it that, was to follow that old axiom: "Buy low and sell high." I thought that meant to buy stocks that were down, figuring that what goes down must go back up. I'd buy big-name companies when they were depressed, because I'd been told, "You can't go wrong with HDIL or Reliance Communication." Buying these stocks when they dropped seemed like a great idea to me back then, because I believed they were less risky and eventually had to go up. Wrong! In time, I learned that there is no such thing as a safe stock. That's like saying there's such a thing as a safe race car. Like race cars, all stocks are risky. However, my lessons came at a cost, as I found myself consistently losing money without a clear understanding of where I was going wrong. These early years in my trading career were marked by uncertainty and financial setbacks. Just because a company is a household name or a well-established business with experienced management doesn't mean it's a great stock to buy. During severe bear markets, even "high-quality" companies can get slaughtered; some even go bankrupt. Imagine the state of people who rode into stocks like Idea, Suzlon and Reliance communication with a soul full of hope! That's more than a 90 percent decline in value! Many years later, investors that bought those stocks were still sitting with a massive percent loss.

To cut a long story short; the turning point came when I immersed myself in an enlightening course on Demand and Supply Strategies, crafted by seasoned Floor Traders at the Chicago Mercantile Exchange, USA. The simplicity and effectiveness of demand and supply trading brought trading back to its fundamental basics. Prior to this, my forays into the market were more akin to gambles than strategic trades, conducted sporadically from my office desk while navigating the challenges of a full-time position in a retail bank.

The stressful nature of my retail banking job was compounded by the rollercoaster ride of watching my investments skyrocket and plummet. It was during this tumultuous period that I realized the crucial factor I had overlooked as a beginner trader—my level of comfort with investment risk. Back then, I lacked the foundational knowledge to assess my own risk tolerance and returns expectations.

Each trade brought a new wave of hope, with every uptick exhilarating and every nosedive equally disheartening. Recognizing that something needed to change, I, like many of you, refused to give up easily. The solution lay in a deep dive into self-education, and that's when the transformative CME's Demand and Supply strategy entered the scene.

While this strategy reshaped my perspective on trading and continues to do so, it also brought to light a critical aspect I had overlooked—my complex relationship with profits and losses — the psychological aspect! Trading, I realized, is meant to be enjoyed, not taken too seriously. To truly relish this game, I discovered two indispensable elements: a) Knowing oneself as a trader and identifying the most suitable trading style, and b) Becoming comfortable with risk and reward through innovative risk calculation and management techniques.

This paradigm shifts not only transformed my trading journey but also led me to reflect on the essence of the game itself. Now, twelve years later, I extend a warm welcome to all new traders, inviting you to partake in the exhilarating world of trading—a journey that promises fulfillment, provided you first understand and embrace the game and, most importantly, know yourself before venturing into the unpredictable realm of Miss Markets!

Happy Learning.
Somraj Dutta
January, 2024, Kolkata

# How To Use This Book

W elcome to **"Trade Smart: The Essential Guide to Psychology & Risk Management"** - your companion on the exciting journey through the intricate world of financial markets. Whether you're a novice trader, an intermediate investor, a student diving into finance, or a seasoned professional, this section will guide you on how to extract the most value from this comprehensive guide.

For Novice Traders and Investors:

If you're new to trading and investing, start with the early chapters. Lay the foundation by understanding the financial success mindset in Chapter 1. Navigate emotional landscapes and cultivate discipline with Chapters 2 and 3. Move progressively through subsequent chapters to build a solid understanding of risk management, market analysis, and the art of resilience.

For Intermediate Traders and Investors:

If you've got some experience under your belt, dive into specific chapters based on your challenges. Strengthen risk management skills in Chapter 4, and refine your trading plan and goal-setting strategies in Chapter 5. Chapters 6 and 7 offer insights into overcoming cognitive biases and making sense of market analysis for smarter choices.

For Trading Psychology Enthusiasts:

Those fascinated by the psychological aspects of trading, delve into Chapters 10 and 15. Master mindfulness, patience, and consistency with practical tips from Chapter 11. Explore the power of trading journals in Chapter 12, and embrace losses for growth in Chapter 13.

For Students and Academia:

Supplement your theoretical knowledge with real-world insights. Relate academic understanding to practical scenarios with case studies provided in each chapter. Connect theories from your classes to tangible strategies presented in the book.

For Long-Term Investors:

Investors seeking a long-term perspective, Chapters 8 and 9 are key. Understand the nuances of long-term investing versus short-term strategies. Embrace resilience, navigate market storms, and balance work, life, and trading in the chapters tailored for enduring success.

For Professionals in Financial Services:

If you're a financial professional, leverage the comprehensive content to enhance your advisory skills. Understand the psychological challenges faced by clients and gain insights into guiding them through market fluctuations.

For Anyone Interested in Financial Literacy:

If you're here for general financial literacy, start with Chapters 1 and 2 to understand the basics. Progress through the book to gain a holistic understanding of trading psychology, market dynamics, and decision-making.

Regardless of your background, remember: your journey to financial success starts here. Each chapter is designed to provide practical tools, actionable insights, and a road-map to navigate the unpredictable seas of financial markets. Let this guide be the wind in your sails, propelling you towards a successful and fulfilling trading journey.

Now, embark on this voyage with an open mind and a hunger for knowledge. Happy reading!

# Contents

# Chapter 1

## Can You Master Your Mind for Successful Trading?

*"The elements of good trading are: (1) cutting losses, (2) cutting losses, and (3) cutting losses. If you can follow these three rules, you may have a chance." — Ed Seykota.*

Welcome to the financial markets! Before you take even the first step in this wild game, remember this golden truth: <u>your mind influences making money.</u> Let me show you how your thoughts and feelings impact trading and investing.

Okay, so let's see how psychology plays a big role in trading and investing. It is not just numbers and charts. Think of the stock market as a battleground. It is a fight between human emotions and behaviors. Let me uncover how our feelings, thoughts, and decision-making shape our financial destinies.

When you put aside the finance stuff, you will see this rollercoaster of emotions that come with market ups and downs. There is ALWAYS a psychological side to our financial choices.

So, why does understanding psychology matter in financial markets? Imagine a map. It not only guides you through a market-labyrinth but also helps you navigate your own mind. That is the key to financial success.

Emotions, usually seen as troublemakers, can actually turn into powerful tools. Like say Fear; if you handle it right, it holds you from making reckless decisions in a downturn. Similarly, Greed, when you understand it, can drive ambition without taking crazy risks. When we explore the psychology of these emotions, it gives us control over our reactions. It also teaches us how to use them smartly.

Understanding psychology also lets us read market sentiments. It gives us an edge, uncovering hidden stories in market trends. Come to think of it as having a superpower in the financial world!

Understanding Emotions in Finance

I know how boring finance classes can be! So let us dive deep and look into feelings and thoughts; we will explore how they play a huge role when we make money decisions! That's why I have made it a point to mix what you learn in this book with real-life situations. This will empower you to handle crazy market times while building a strong mindset for financial success.

In short, this is a book where we connect numbers of stories and emotions. Because winning isn't just about what you know but also who you are, right? Let's start this journey into the psychology of trading—a sojourn where knowledge meets gut feelings, and success comes from not just financial smarts but also from having the right mindset.

Emotions, when harnessed correctly, become powerful tools in trading decision.

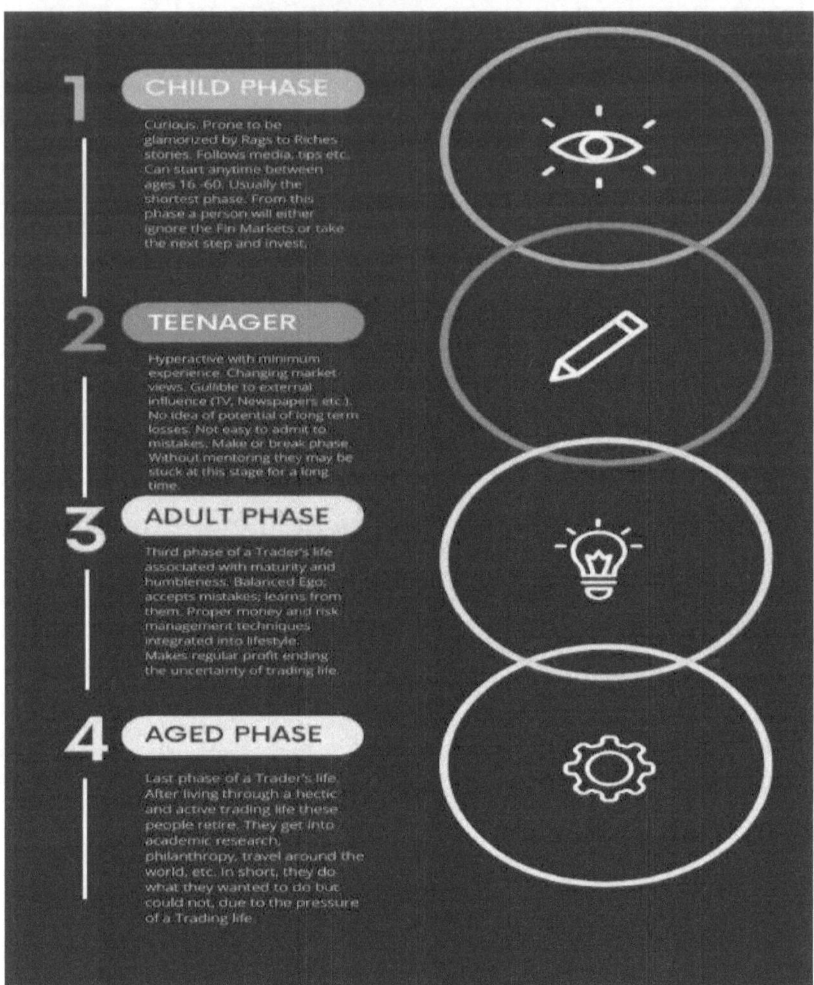


*Trader's Life Cycle*

Note: Most traders cannot move out of the teenager stage because of one simple reason: they do not implement money and Risk Management in their trading journey. As a Trader, you must have realized that you have no control over the market and it is impossible for anybody to predict the price movements. However, you have absolute control over your trading account, and how you manage your money will decide your future as a trader.

Key Points:

1. Mind significantly influences making money in financial markets.

2. Psychology plays a crucial role in trading beyond numerical analysis.

3. Emphasize the emotional ride accompanying market fluctuations.

4. Understanding psychology is the key to navigating market complexities and achieving financial success.

# Chapter 2

# How Can You Master the Secrets of Trading Emotions?

*"You have to learn how to lose; it is more important than learning how to win." — Mark Weinstein*

We all feel angry, greedy, or impulsive. Emotions are a big deal here, shaping how traders make decisions and plan their strategies. This chapter will break down the emotional rollercoaster in trading and giving you tip on handling it.

Let's talk about three main emotions in trading:

Fear, Greed, and Hope.

Think of the stock market as a wild sea, and these emotions are the winds guiding or messing up traders' journeys.

Emotions aren't just sitting on the sidelines; they're actively driving decision-making. Unchecked fear and greed can lead to snap decisions that mess up a trader's overall game plan. It's crucial to spot these emotional triggers so you can handle your reactions like a pro.

So, how do you manage emotions like a 'Boss'? Trading is like mastering yourself. You need clear rules, rational thinking, and constant self-awareness. Balancing your feelings with logical analysis helps you stay cool and adjust your strategies as the market changes.

In a nutshell, recognizing, understanding, and handling emotions aren't optional for successful traders. Yes, read that again, I mean it. Fear, greed, and hope will always be a part of the market ride, but those who can ride these emotional waves will bring confidence and resilience to the game. They are the real winners.

Case Study:
Mastering the Emotional Landscape

Meet Sarah, a novice trader enthusiastic about making her mark in the financial markets. Excitement and hope fuel her initial trades, but soon she encounters the turbulent sea of emotions affecting her decision-making.

Fear, the Tempest:

Sarah experiences her first significant loss, triggering fear. Panic sets in, leading her to hastily sell off investments to cut losses. This knee-jerk reaction results in missed opportunities for recovery.

Greed, the Siren Song:

In the subsequent weeks, a series of profitable trades boost Sarah's confidence. However, greed takes the helm as she becomes overconfident, increasing trade sizes without proper risk management. The inevitable market correction leaves her with substantial losses.

Hope, the Guiding Star:

Undeterred, Sarah holds on to losing positions, hoping for a miraculous turnaround. This emotional attachment blinds her to market realities, further amplifying her losses.

Navigating the Emotional Storm

Learning from her emotional rollercoaster, Sarah turns the tide:

Fear Management:

Implementing a strategic risk management plan with stop-loss orders to limit potential losses and prevent fear-driven impulsive decisions.

Greed Checks:

Adopting a disciplined approach with predefined profit-taking targets and avoiding aggressive over-leveraging to curb the influence of greed.

Reality-Based Hope

Shifting focus from unrealistic optimism to realistic expectations, embracing losses as opportunities for growth, and aligning hope with informed decision-making.

Through mindfulness, emotional discipline, and a new-found understanding of her emotional landscape, Sarah transforms from a reactive trader to a resilient and informed market participant. This case study illustrates the practical application of emotional intelligence in navigating the complexities of trading.

**Key Points:**

1. There is a profound impact of emotions on traders' decisions and strategies.

2. Identify fear, greed, and hope as central emotions influencing traders' experiences in the market.

3. The stock market is like a turbulent sea, with emotions acting as guiding winds for traders.

4. Emotions play an active role in driving decision-making and the importance of recognizing triggers.

5. To develop self-mastery in trading have clear rules, use rational thinking, with continuous self-awareness to balance emotions with logical analysis.

# Chapter 3

# Do Emotions Drive Trading Success?

*"Trading doesn't just reveal your character; it also builds it if you stay in the game long enough."* - *Yvan Byeajee*

I magine a typical trading floor - you witness some of sort of 'madness' - traders screaming over each other trying to navigate this crazy world (technically this age–old process was named "Open Outcry" - which is on its way out in the wake of Digitalization!). Make no mistake but keeping a cool head is your secret weapon against market craziness. Professional Traders do just that.

Here I would like to help you build up emotional discipline, so you can make smart decisions without getting swept away by the chaos.

Let's break down some simple yet powerful techniques for managing your emotions in the trading game:

Take a Risk Assessment Test:
Many Investment Advisors can guide you through this important test. It's the crucial first step to understanding yourself. This test helps you figure out your comfort level with risk and how much uncertainty you can handle in case of a loss.

The Risk Assessment Test (RAT) also uncovers your preferred trading style. If you find that you have a low tolerance for risk, consider trading for the longer term (like myself, for example!). Keep your investments in place while using charts and fundamental analysis to guide your decisions. On the other hand, if you're comfortable with a higher level of risk, diving into the active trading world, like Intraday trading, might be a suitable option. This could be a good fit if you're not the patient type and prefer more immediate results. Ultimately, it's all about understanding yourself and your preferences

Note: I've added a useful "test" for you to check your score. You can use it for a self-assessment.

Set Personal Rules:

Create rules for yourself when you trade, like deciding your risk and reward levels. For example, you might set profit targets or use stop losses. When you finally browse through the annexures to this book you will find some very interesting Personal Rules which I personally use till today. This will set you in the right path and help you avoid some common mistakes Traders perform without planning.

## RULES ARE MEANINGLESS WITHOUT DISCIPLINE

It's no good having a "mental stop"—telling yourself, if the stock falls to "X" I will get out there—if you don't follow it. That's like driving without ever using the brakes or, only using them on occasion. The problem with a mental stop is that it's too easy to "forget," and then hold onto a losing trade, telling yourself that you'll sell once the stock recovers. Let me get back to breakeven and I'll get out. The stock may keep going lower, while the loss keeps getting bigger. For most traders, it becomes even harder to sell as a loss balloons. Every huge loss starts as a small one. The only way to protect a trade from turning into a large loss is to accept a small loss before it snowballs out of control.

Importance of having Stop Losses:

I've heard some pundits say trading with a stoploss is foolish! Only a fool would make such a statement! Trading without a stop-loss is like driving a car without brakes. Maybe you could make it around the block a few times, but if you did drive without brakes, how far do you think you could go before you crash? The same holds true for trading: when you fail to trade with stop-loss protection, you are absolutely guaranteed to have a major accident; it's just a matter of time.

What if things don't go as planned? Then your plan must account for negative developments. The reality is you will have many trades that do not work out as you expected. You must have a plan to deal with those situations and minimize the damage. You should know the signs that a trade is problematic, which can tip you off it's time to exit the stock or reduce your position—in some cases even before it hits your stop. Maybe the stock's fundamentals deteriorate. Or maybe it's a good company, but your timing was off and a better technical setup will emerge later. But as for the trade you're in right now, if your expectations are not being met and the stock is not acting right, you need to recognize it.

Pick the Right Market Conditions:

Avoid trading in unfavourable market conditions. If you're not feeling confident or the market isn't right, it's okay to step away. Don't rely on trading to boost your mood.

Adjust Your Trade Size:

To keep your emotions in check, try trading smaller amounts. For example, if you began with a $10,000 account and initially traded the whole $10,000, think about cutting it down to a set percentage, like 1–2%. This way, you're setting a fixed risk against at least twice the potential reward (2:1). It helps minimize stress and lowers the chance of significant losses, avoiding putting all your eggs in one trade basket. You can start trading higher amounts as your confidence picks up.

Have a Trading Plan and Journal: Without a plan, you can only rationalize. Often you will tell yourself to be patient when you should be selling, or you may panic during a natural pullback and then miss out on a huge stock move.

Develop a trading plan to prepare for different outcomes, especially around significant news events. Traders who use plans and keep journals tend to handle emotions better. Trading is serious business with real money on the line. Why would you go into it without a well-thought-out plan of action? Yet, most people do. The ease of entry into the stock market—no license or training required; just open a brokerage account and go—may give people the false impression that trading is easy. Or, perhaps they think their odds of succeeding without much thought are far better than they really are. Whatever the reason, I've seen people invest $100,000 in a stock with less research than when they buy an $700 flat screen TV. They'll commit thousands of dollars to a stock because of a tip from a friend of a friend, without spending much time if any on research and planning. Greed takes over, and all they can see is the upside, without much thought about the downside or if the unthinkable happens!

Your goal as a stock speculator is preparedness, to trade with few surprises. To do so, you need to develop a dependable way to handle virtually every situation that may occur. Preparation is the key! Till today before I make a trade, I have already worked out responses to meet virtually any conceivable development that may take place.

While preparing a Trading Plan here are some priorities in Order of Importance:

a. Limit your loss. Define how much you're willing to risk and set a stop-loss.

b. Protect your line. Once the stock price moves up and you have a decent profit (generally after the first natural reaction and a recovery to new highs), you should then move up the stop near your breakeven point.

c. Protect your profit. Don't allow good-size gains to slip away; use a trailing stop or a back stop.

Stay Relaxed: Like I mentioned at the Introduction –Enjoy your trading, and stay relaxed. When you're calm, you can make more rational decisions in any market situation.

Deep Breathing: Take deliberate deep breaths to stay calm amid market ups and downs. It's a quick and effective way to reduce stress and think clearly.

Mindfulness Practices: Stay in the moment during trades. Mindfulness helps you step back from emotional reactions, so you can watch market movements with a clear head.

Visualization: Picture success in your mind to ease anxiety and boost confidence. It's like creating a mental roadmap for a positive and proactive mindset. Creating a vision is very crucial.

Establishing Rituals:Establish pre-trading habits to get your mind ready for trading. This helps you stay focused and in the right mindset. While I won't dive deep into pre-trading rituals here, as they vary among traders, I recommend exploring and learning more about them online. You can also consider joining a comprehensive Trading and Investment course for a more in-depth understanding

Incorporating Calming Exercises: Whether it's a quick meditation or some stretching, calming exercises keep your nerves in check. They act as a buffer against emotional ups and downs, so you enter the market composed and collected.

Preventing Impulsive/ Rash Reactions: Emotional discipline acts like a shield, preventing you from making rash decisions when things get wild. Stick to your strategies and stay in control.

Rational Decisions in Volatility: Emotional discipline helps you make logical decisions, preventing big losses and positioning yourself strategically during market ups and downs.

In a nutshell, emotional discipline is the key to success in the intricate world of trading. The techniques we've covered here are like a toolbox for mastering your emotions. By using these practices, you're not just mastering the markets; you're mastering yourself on the go!

**Case Study:**

The Calm Captain

Enter Alex, an aspiring trader navigating the stormy seas of market volatility. In Chapter 3, Alex learns the art of emotional discipline, transforming into the calm captain of their trading ship.

Market Turbulence: Alex encounters a sudden market downturn, triggering anxiety and impulsive reactions. The emotional storm threatens to jeopardize their trading journey.

Implementing Practical Techniques: Alex embraces the power of deep breathing and mindfulness. Establishing a pre-trading routine becomes the compass, providing stability amidst market chaos.

Weathering Emotional Ups and Downs: Calming exercises and a structured routine act as buffers against emotional turbulence. Alex learns to maintain composure, preventing impulsive reactions.

Discipline as the North Star: Emotional discipline emerges as the key to preventing reactive decision-making. By adhering to a routine and incorporating calming exercises, Alex fortifies against the emotional ups and downs of trading.

Building Resilience Against Market Tempests

Alex's journey reflects the importance of emotional discipline:

Cool Composure: Alex cultivates cool composure, transforming emotional reactions into calculated responses during market storms.

Mindful Techniques:

Incorporating mindfulness and pre-trading routines to create a focused mindset, ensuring a disciplined approach in the face of market uncertainties.

Stability Amidst Chaos:

Building resilience becomes paramount for Alex. The ability to weather market cycles and maintain composure during turbulent times contributes to personal growth.

Alex's evolution from a reactive trader to a resilient captain showcases the practical application of emotional discipline, offering valuable insights for readers navigating their own trading voyages.

Key Points:

1. Cool composure is a trader's secret weapon against market chaos.

2. Practical techniques like deep breathing and mindfulness aid in managing emotions.

3. Building a pre-trading routine signals focus and stability.

4. Incorporating calming exercises acts as a buffer against emotional ups and downs.

5. Emotional discipline is crucial for preventing impulsive reactions, making rational decisions, and achieving success in trading.

# Chapter 4

# Can Strategic Discipline Transform Your Risk into Reward?

*"The goal of a successful trader is to make the best trades. Money is secondary." - Alexander Elder*

In trading, every decision counts. We're now diving into the skills that'll help you navigate the unpredictable waters of financial markets. Let me call it 'The Trading Tightrope.'

Trading is like a dance where you balance between risk and reward. Each trade involves a calculated risk for a potential reward. Picture walking on a tightrope - the challenge is to stay balanced. Successful traders know how to balance potential profit and possible loss in each trade. For instance, if the potential profit is $500 and the potential loss is $100, it's a 1:5 risk–reward ratio. This balance is key for long-term success. Conversely when you turn the ratio around it shows you Reward for every unit of Risk taken - it helps you consider whether or not the benefits really do outweigh the cost.

Having a positive risk–reward ratio isn't just a strategy; it's a mindset. It means understanding that losses are part of the journey, but what matters is ensuring wins are more than losses. Like any business a Professional Trader treats her Trading like a business and hence is okay with 'Net Profits'.

It's also time we tell you how to set "Stop Losses" - think of it as building protective walls for your castle. Traders use stop–loss orders to prevent significant losses. It's like having defensive walls around your fortress. By setting levels at which a trade will automatically close, traders shield themselves from big losses during unpredictable market conditions.

Following risk management plans is like having a battle strategy. It involves setting clear rules on how much money to risk, spreading investments, and regularly reviewing and adjusting your risk plan. This way, traders not only protect their money but also make sure that one bad trade doesn't harm their entire portfolio.

Like I had mentioned before: Financial markets are like stormy seas, full of unpredictable waves. In this ever-changing environment, remember for life, that: discipline is the steering wheel that guides the ship.

Sticking to the plan during market changes is tough, I know, but it is vital. Make no mistakes about this. It means resisting emotional trading when markets are turbulent. Discipline keeps traders on track. It's about sticking to the plan, even when the markets try to push them off course. I ought to add in here that individual plans to trade will vary. It is a whole new subject which will call for a separate book so let's not discuss much depth here.

But do not confuse discipline with being too strict; It's about being flexible within a framework. It means understanding that markets change, and strategies might need adjustments, but the core principles stay firm. Discipline acts like an anchor, which can prevent you from being swept away by the market's movements - which you definitely do NOT want!

In conclusion, risk and discipline are the foundations of successful trading. They work together to create a strong and profitable trading journey. Balancing risk and reward, protecting against losses, and staying disciplined during market changes are the keys to sail through the volatile markets.

**Case Study:**

The Risk-Averse Maverick

Meet Sarah, an adventurous trader exploring the dynamic dance between risk and reward in Chapter 4. Her journey unfolds as she embraces the art of strategic risk management.

Balancing Act:

Sarah views trading as a balanced dance, understanding that risk and reward are inseparable partners. She seeks equilibrium, recognizing that a cautious approach can lead to sustainable success.

Stop-Loss Orders as Defenses:

Sarah learns to wield stop-loss orders as shields against significant losses. These strategic tools become her arsenal for protecting capital in the unpredictable market terrain.

Advocating Discipline:

Discipline becomes Sarah's guiding star. She rigorously adheres to clear rules and conducts regular reviews. This disciplined approach acts as a compass, ensuring she stays on course through market changes.

Navigating Market Changes:

Sarah concludes that risk and discipline are the bedrock of successful trading. The ability to navigate market changes with a disciplined mindset positions her as a maverick in the trading arena.

Foundations of Successful Trading:
Risk and Discipline

Sarah's journey exemplifies the essence of Chapter 4:

Balanced Decision–Making: Sarah's approach involves a harmonious blend of risk and reward, showcasing the significance of a balanced trading strategy.

Strategic Defense:

Introduction of stop–loss orders empowers Sarah to defend against substantial losses, emphasizing the importance of proactive risk management.

Discipline as the Cornerstone:

Sarah advocates for discipline as the cornerstone of successful trading, demonstrating its role in navigating the ever–changing market landscape.

Adaptability: Sarah's ability to adapt to market changes while maintaining discipline establishes her as a risk-averse maverick.

Readers embarking on their trading adventures can draw inspiration from Sarah's strategic risk management, gaining valuable insights for crafting their own path to success.

Key Points:

1. Describes trading as a balanced dance between risk and reward.

2. Introduces stop-loss orders as defences against significant losses.

3. Emphasizes strategic risk management with clear rules and regular reviews.

4. Advocates discipline as crucial for navigating market changes.

5. Concludes with risk and discipline as the foundation of successful trading.

**Enjoying the journey to financial success with this book? Your positive reviews can inspire others to embark on this transformative experience. Share your thoughts, insights, and the impact this book has had on your trading journey. Your**

review is not just a reflection of your experience; it's a beacon guiding fellow traders towards success. Thank you.

# Chapter 5

---

# Trading Blueprint: Key to Financial Triumph?

*"Most traders take a good system and destroy it by trying to make it into a perfect system." – Robert Prechter*

In this chapter, we're diving into the basics of creating a killer trading plan and realistic goals. Success in financial markets isn't luck; it's about smart planning.

Crafting a Trading Plan: Your Guide to Success

Your trading plan is like your best buddy in trading. It's not just a bunch of rules; it's a personalized guide that tells you what to do when you feel lost or confused or both.

Defining Entry and Exit Strategies: Your Roadmap for Trades

Think of entering the financial markets without a plan like going on a road trip without a map. It's risky. A good trading plan spells out when to get in and out of trades, giving you a structured way to handle the market.

Planning Position Sizes: Managing Risks and Gaining Consistent Gains

I briefly alluded to this in a previous chapter. We will call "Risk-Management" the guardian of your money. Your plan should say how much of your money you're willing to risk on each trade. This creates a safety net to protect you from big losses.

Ideally the size of your positions should be very conservative. If is very easy to be swayed by the high profit potential of large positions especially while trading derivatives. If you have $1000 in your trading account and you a thousand shares at a market price of $100/ share, you will lose all your capital by just a $1 move against you! On the other hand, if you buy just a hundred shares, you can be relaxed as it would require $10 decline (i.e. a 10% reduction in the original share price) before you lose all your money. Of course, this situation will not arise in practical cases since you will definitely but putting a stop loss. Looking from this point of view, you can sustain 10 stop losses of $1 each if you buy hundred shares instead of thousand.

Consider this:

1. Initial Risk Capital:

Begin your trading journey with an initial capital of $5,000.

2. Intraday Trading:

Risk Appetite @ 1%: Choose a conservative approach, risking $25 per trade for intraday trading.

Maximum Risk (Intraday):

Set a monthly cap of $1,000 for a total of 50 intraday trades over 20 days.

Total Intraday Trades: Plan to execute 40 trades.
Account Positions: Maintain two open positions simultaneously.
Risk Per Trade: Each intraday trade carries a risk of $25.

3. Swing Trading:

Risk Appetite @ 2%: Opt for a slightly higher risk, with $50 per trade for swing trading.

Maximum Risk
(Swing):
Set a monthly limit of $2,000 for a total of 40 swing trades over 20 days.

Total Swing Trades: Aim to execute 80 trades.
Account Positions: Keep four open positions concurrently.

Risk Per Trade: Each swing trade involves a risk of $50.

4. Total Risk Management:

Maximum Total Risk/Month: Limit the overall risk exposure to $3,000.

Maximum Total Risk in 6 Months: Ensure the cumulative risk does not surpass $18,000.

Total Trades Possible in a Month: You can execute a maximum of 120 trades monthly.

These rules serve as your guiding principles to navigate the complexities of risk in trading. By adhering to these clear guidelines, you not only protect your capital but also establish a disciplined and sustainable approach to your trading journey. Remember, managing risk is about safeguarding your assets and ensuring lasting success in the dynamic world of financial markets.

Now, consider a Day Trader. Her goal might involve reaching a specific weekly monetary target. To figure this out, she'd look at not only the total trades planned, but also the expected win rate (overall probability of hits to misses), the average value of wins to losses. This brings a certain predictability of not only her income but also a horizon by which she can expect such cash flows.

Setting Direction and Focus: Achieving Success with Goals

Think of your trading goals as checkpoints on your financial journey. Each goal guides your decisions and keeps you on the path to success, whether it's monthly gains or long-term wealth accumulation.

Creating a Roadmap for Decision-Making: Your GPS in Trading

Goals act like destinations on a map. The clearer your goals, the easier it is to navigate. Remember: Clarity creates power; setting clear and achievable goals is like creating a roadmap for your trading journey. It outlines the steps needed to reach each goal, providing a structured approach to decision-making.

Adapting Plans to Market Conditions: Navigating the Market's Changes

Change is another name of the financial markets - always with its own ebbs and turns. A successful trader adapts to these shifts not fight with them.

Adjusting Plans Based on Market Shifts: Staying Flexible

Your trading plan should be flexible, letting you navigate shifts in the market. Being able to adapt to new opportunities or shield yourself from risks requires flexibility. Like for example when successful traders trade, they mix defensive (companies that are not usually perturbed by market conditions given their essential goods at sale etc.) with cyclical stocks (seasonal with ups and down or subject to market cycles) to produce a buffer or they may take go long on a surging market while going short on a bearish sector - it's all a matter of individual strategy for protecting yourself from the downsides.

Regular Reviews for Better Alignment: Refining Strategies

Regularly checking your trading plan helps you figure out what's working and what needs tweaking. It ensures your strategies match the current market conditions.

In a nutshell, success in trading is a journey, not a destination. Your trading plan and goals are your guides, helping you navigate the twists and turns of financial markets. Embrace the dynamic nature of the markets, adapt your strategies, and let your goals be the constant guiding light on your path to financial success. Keep in mind that a net loss on your income statement for a specific day doesn't signify the conclusion of that day, especially when your perspective is based on a monthly outlook. It's essentially about ensuring your goals are in sync with your timelines.

Develop a Trading System:

This is simply a set of parameters and rules that govern your entry and exit positions. Once you have learnt all the technical tools, you will come up with your favorite ones that work for you. For example, you may develop a simple "buy" system when a 13-day moving average crosses above the 21-day moving average with an increase in Volume. Once this happens you will buy the security no matter what your emotions are and what other traders are saying. Remember that it is neither possible nor profitable to use too many tools; therefore your trading system should be simple consisting of only three to four trading parameters. Stick to the system that you have developed. The majority of the Traders I have interviewed who failed did so just by not sticking to a single strategy. Stick to your system; refine it with each trading experience and try to remove the shortcomings. Look for a different trading system only when you are sure that the system had been given adequate time and energy, but still failed to generate expected profits. If you have to be a successful trader, you must devote your energy in finding trading techniques that work for you and not focus on invidual trades as a benchmark for success or failure.

You should keep the following points in mind while developing a trading system.

Key Components of a Trading System:

A. Liquidity: Your trading systems should be developed and tested on markets with high liquidity. Equity indices, four major currency pairs, gold and crude oil in commodities are perfect for developing a trading system. If you are a stock trader, remember that no trading system can be developed for a low volume and illiquid stocks. The same applies for rarely-trades commodities and currency pairs too.

B. Risk Controls:
Your system should have adequate measures to control risk. The stop loss levels should be decided before entry into a trade, and it should be adhered to. The stop loss should not be too far away from the entry price, as the wide gap will finish your account within a few trades. In my trading course and classes I teach my students to put stop losses levels mechanically as a certain percentage of the Average True Range. The meaures vary with trading style. Which means a Swing Traders will follow a different set of SL rules than a Day Trader.

C. System Should be Profitable:

You must include all costs associated with trading such as brokerage, taxes, etc. to look at system profitably.

D. System Should be Consistent:

Your system should show consistent profits. It does not mean that you should get an increasing number of increasing profits; rather, even there are strings of losses, the profits should be able to cover all those losses within a set time-frame.

Note: Almost all software now a days have the facility to create an automated trading system. Once you program the system, "Buy" and "Sell" will be indicated automatically whenever a particular condition is met. This is also known as mechanical trading. This helps you to back-test your system but do not rely too much on back-testing.

Much better is trading on "Paper" (*hypothetical trading process) or buying and selling single shares! Gradually increase your bets as you gain confidence over your system. Real trading will give your exact results and writted records with all costs included. You you get a feel of the real thing. Try it out. You have nothing to lose but a whole new world to gain.

Managing the Risk:

As stated by Bruce Kovner, an American billionaire hedge fund manager,

"I know where I'm getting out before I get in. Whenever I enter a position, I have a predetermined stop. That is the only way I can sleep. The position size on a trade is determined by the stop, and the stop is determined on a technical basis"

Hence, you must remember this: RESPECT YOUR STOP LOSS.

Even the greatest trader incur some losses from time to time. It is an integral aspect of being a trader. Idea is to limit your losses to a more manageable level. Thus you will be able to remain in the market longer, boosting your chances of making more profitable trades.

For this I always mention to my students to adhere to a minimum 2:1 or even 3:1 Reward to Risk ratio. Your targetted gains should be at least twice your maximum losses. If you adhere to this R:R Ratio you only require 2 wins to go into profit even when you are incurring 3 losses. I am not saying it is a general rule but this may help you visualize a particular risk management strategy.

Let us look at an illustration to show this. Two traders both begin with $10,000 and use a 2:1 reward-to-risk ratio, but they are using vastly different levels of Risk management. The first trader uses a very aggressive strategy, risking 60% of her money on each transaction and aiming for a 120% profit. The second trader is far more conservative. He risks just 5% of his account size while pursuing at least a 10% reward per trade. For the sake of simplicity let us assume both performs 10 trades each where every second trade becomes profitable (assumption).

I have outlined the effectiveness of the strategy in the next page. Have a look and decide for yourself who did what. You will clearly understand what I'm trying to indicate here.

| Period | Capital | Profit + 120% | Loss -60% | Period | Capital | Profit + 10% | Loss -5% |
|---|---|---|---|---|---|---|---|
| 0 | $10000 | | | 0 | $10000 | | |
| 1 | $22,000 | $12000 | | 1 | $11,000 | $1000 | |
| 2 | $8800 | | -$13200 | 2 | $10450 | | -$550 |
| 3 | $19360 | $10560 | | 3 | $11495 | $1045 | |
| 4 | $7744 | | -$11616 | 4 | $10920 | | -$575 |
| 5 | $17037 | $9293 | | 5 | $12012 | $1092 | |
| 6 | $6815 | | -$10222 | 6 | $11412 | | -$600 |
| 7 | $14992 | $8187 | | 7 | $12553 | $1141 | |
| 8 | $5997 | | -$8995 | 8 | $11925 | | -$628 |
| 9 | $13193 | $7196 | | 9 | $13118 | $1193 | |
| 10 | $5277 | | -$7916 | 10 | $12462 | | -$656 |

The table above captures the core of idea of risk management. Two separate sets of performances with different degrees of risk management.

Despite the fact that both methods had similar success rates, the ultimate outcomes are remarkably different due to the significantly different money management approaches. The first trader's aggressive allocation of Risk Capital per trade resulted in a net loss of 47%, whereas the prudent second trader sailed right into profitability ($12,462) at 25%!. Did you notice how a little tweak in your risk management strategy can dramatically improve profits?

An expert trader understands how much he or she can risk, but as a novice, you should do everything in your power to avoid heavy losses. Yes, losses will always remain an integral part of your (trading) business, but it is crucial to know how to deal with them. Management Profit is another aspect. So there should be a mathematically positive balance between the two possible outcomes of a trade: maximizing profit while minimizing loss.

**Case Study:**

The Strategic Navigator

Meet Alex, a meticulous trader navigating the financial universe with a personalized trading plan in Chapter 5. Alex's journey exemplifies the importance of a structured approach to decision-making.

Personalized Trading Plan:

Alex, armed with a tailored trading plan, embarks on a journey akin to sailing through financial waters. The plan acts as a compass, providing direction and focus in the vast sea of market opportunities.

Clear Entry and Exit Strategies: Alex likens trading without a plan to a risky journey. By defining clear entry and exit strategies, Alex ensures a smoother voyage, minimizing the uncertainties associated with aimless navigation.

Risk Management as a Guiding Star:

Introducing risk management, Alex defines the amount of money to risk on each trade. This calculated approach positions risk management as a guiding star, offering stability and consistency in the financial universe.

Flexible Plans for Dynamic Markets:

Alex underscores the significance of flexible plans that adapt to market shifts. Regular reviews and strategy refinement become integral components of Alex's trading voyage, ensuring adaptability in dynamic market conditions.

Key Takeaways for Aspiring Traders: Crafting Your Path to Financial Success

Blueprint for Decision-Making: Alex's journey emphasizes the importance of a personalized trading plan as a blueprint for informed decision-making.

Reducing Uncertainties: Clear entry and exit strategies act as navigational aids, reducing uncertainties in the ever-changing financial seas.

Guidance through Risk Management: Risk management serves as a guiding star, providing stability and direction in the tumultuous world of trading.

Adaptability in Strategy: Alex's flexible approach showcases the necessity of adapting plans to market shifts, ensuring resilience in the face of dynamic conditions.

Key Points:

1. Emphasizes the importance of a personalized trading plan for decision-making.

2. Compares trading without a plan to a risky journey, stressing the need for clear entry and exit strategies.

3. Introduces risk management as crucial, defining the amount of money to risk on each trade.

4. Positions goals as guiding stars, offering direction and focus in the financial universe.

5. Highlights the significance of flexible plans, adapting to market shifts, and regular reviews for strategy refinement.

# Chapter 6

## Beat Bias, Trade Better: Possible?

*"If you can learn to create a state of mind that is not affected by the market's behaviour, the struggle will cease to exist." –Mark Douglas*

Don't get too nervous hearing words like: 'Cognitive Biases' etc. In simple terms these are the games our mind plays with us.

When you are in the Markets, making 'smart decisions' is the key to success. But guess what? Our brains have some quirks that can mess with our trading game. Let me break down these common quirks, how they mess with trading, and ways to outsmart them.

Let's dive into the biases that can trip us up:

Confirmation Bias: The Allure of Affirmation

What it means: Giving more weight to info that agrees with what you already think.

Example: You like a tech company, so you only look for news that says it's great.

Fix: Search for info that disagrees with you. Question your thoughts and analysis.

Anchoring Bias: The Weight of Initial Impressions

What it means: Relying too much on the first info you get.

Example: An investor buys shares of a tech company at $100 per share. Subsequently, the stock experiences a temporary dip due to market fluctuations and is now priced at $80 per share. Despite positive long-term prospects for the company, the investor remains fixated on the initial $100 price, anchoring their perception.

Fix: Reevaluate the info and look at the bigger picture. Don't get stuck on the first bits of data.

Herd Mentality: Following the Crowd

What it means: Going along with the big group without thinking.

Example: If a popular stock suddenly experiences a surge in buying activity, investors might join in without fully understanding the reasons behind the price movement. This behaviour can lead to inflated stock prices based on collective sentiment rather than fundamental factors, and it often results in increased market volatility.

Fix: Stay independent. Think for yourself, analyze the market, and make decisions based on your own research.

Now, let's tackle these biases head-on with some strategies:

Question Assumptions and Seek Contradictory Evidence: The Power of Skepticism

How to fight biases:

Be skeptical. Question your beliefs and actively look for info that challenges them. Get info from different sources for a well-rounded view.

Take a Step Back: Analyze Decisions with a Rational Approach

How to stay sharp:

When things get crazy, take a breather. Analyze decisions calmly. Consider the big economic picture and how it affects assets.

My Best Advice:

Develop a Checklist: A Systematic Approach to Decision-Making

Stay on track: Make a checklist to keep your decisions in check. Include important factors before making choices, so you have a structured and rational approach.

Here's a typical checklist I employ for my decisions in buying and selling long-term positions. Yours may vary, but this serves as a guide to encourage similar strategic thinking, providing an anchor for your decision-making processes:

Selection and Screening of Stocks based on Fundamental Analysis

Keeping yourself updated on Economic developments and determining the Phase of the Economic cycle

1. Review the following economic indicators on www.tra dingeconomics.com on a monthly basis:

a) IIP
b) GDP

c) PMI

d) Inflation

e) Interest rates

f) Money Supply (shown as M3 in the indicators)

g) Gross Fixed Capital Formation

h) Government & Public Spending

i) Trade Deficit

j) Current Account deficit

k) Fiscal Deficit

l) External Debt

Note: Check the economic calendar on monthly basis to keep myself up-to-date on the trend of the above indicators and predict the possible interest rate scenario which could unfold

2. Use Market outlook Reports or Other brokerage economic reports

3. (other)

Shortlist Sectors

4. My preferred approach for sector analysis would be (Please tick):

a) Use Sector rotation chart

b) Reading a Good Stock report from a good Financial House

c) Attend Investing Live Market Sessions with my Broker; Attend Earnings calls of companies.

d) All of the above

e) (other)

Shortlist Companies

5. Scan for stock ideas based on sectors shortlisted above using (Please tick):

a) www.screener.in

b) Investment Magazines

c) Both of the above

d) Analyze and Review Broker calls where applicable

e) (other)

And/ Or focus on the Power of Now: A journey to self-awareness and mindfulness.

Recognizing and beating biases is an ongoing adventure. Our brains love biases, so it takes some effort to navigate this world successfully.

**Case Study:**

Mindful Mastery

Introducing Sarah, a disciplined trader who delves into the complexities of cognitive biases in Chapter 6, advocating for a mindful approach to decision-making.

Understanding Cognitive Biases:

Sarah simplifies cognitive biases, recognizing their impact on smart trading decisions. Through relatable examples, she breaks down confirmation bias, anchoring, and herd mentality, providing insights into the pitfalls of biased thinking.

Rational Analysis and Questioning Assumptions:

Sarah advocates for strategies like skepticism, rational analysis, and questioning assumptions to counteract cognitive biases. By incorporating a systematic decision-making approach through a checklist, she empowers traders to navigate the intricate web of biases.

Self-Awareness and Mindfulness:

Sarah introduces self-awareness and mindfulness as crucial elements for overcoming biases in professional trading and investing. Through mindfulness exercises, she guides traders, especially students, in cultivating a heightened awareness of their thoughts and biases.

Checklist for Trading:

Sarah presents a simple yet effective checklist for trading decisions. She demonstrates how students can systematically evaluate potential biases, fostering a mindful and disciplined approach to trading.

Key Takeaways for Aspiring Traders: Overcoming Cognitive Biases

Awareness of Biases: Sarah's journey emphasizes the importance of recognizing and understanding cognitive biases as a prerequisite for smart trading decisions.

Counteracting Biases: Rational analysis, skepticism, and questioning assumptions serve as effective strategies to counteract biases, enabling traders to make more objective decisions.

Mindfulness in Decision-Making: Sarah introduces mindfulness and self-awareness as tools to enhance decision-making. Mindful traders are better equipped to navigate biases and make informed choices.

Practical Checklist: The quantitative checklist for trading decisions provides students with a tangible and practical tool to implement Sarah's strategies in real-world trading scenarios.

Key Points:

1. Simplifies cognitive biases, stressing their impact on smart trading decisions.

2. Breaks down confirmation, anchoring, and herd mentality biases with examples.

3. Advocates strategies like scepticism, rational analysis, and questioning assumptions.

4. Recommends a systematic decision-making approach through a checklist for trading.

5. Introduces self-awareness and mindfulness as crucial elements for overcoming biases in professional trading and investing.

# Chapter 7

# Navigating Markets: Can Analysis Unlock Better Decisions?

*"I have two basic rules about winning in trading and in life: 1. If you don't bet, you can't win. 2. If you lose all your chips, you can't bet."* – *Larry Hite*

In this chapter, we're going to break down how to make savvy investing choices without getting all complicated. Cool? Let's dive in!

Different Ways to Look at Markets: Unveiling the Info Layers

Fundamental Analysis: Figuring Out a Company's DNA

Think of it like checking out a company's DNA. We're taking a peek at its financial health by looking at income statements, balance sheets, and cash flow statements (for more on these, you can refer to some of my other books, which makes them super easy to understand). Also, keep an eye on bigger trends by checking out stuff like GDP growth rates and unemployment figures.

Technical Analysis: Decoding Chart Language

This is like understanding a language written in charts and patterns. Analysts here believe that past price and volume data can help predict future market movements. They use tools like moving averages and the Relative Strength Index (RSI) (you can check some of my other books on these topics for easy understanding) to find trends and potential reversal points.

Sentiment Analysis: Feeling the Market's Vibes

The market is like this living organism with feelings! Sentiment analysis is about getting to this mood of the markets by checking out things like surveys, social media trends, and other indicators of public opinion. It's like reading the market's emotional vibe.

Tools for Doing Market Analysis

Indicators for Technical Analysis: Navigating the Price Maze

Technical analysts use countless tools, more popularly moving averages and the RSI to understand market prices. I can't go more detail here, as it's beyond the scope of this book. Just know that these tools work like a compass and map, helping analysts figure out market movements.

Economic Calendars and Earnings Reports: Fundamental Pillars

Fundamental analysts rely on economic calendars and earnings reports. Economic calendars show schedules of economic events, giving insights into broader economic trends. Earnings reports reveal a company's financial performance, acting like a financial compass pointing investors in the right direction.

Market Sentiment Tools: Reading the Collective Mind

To understand this collective consciousness is crucial. Tools like surveys and social media trends help gauge the market sentiment. They act like a microscope that magnifies the collective feelings of investors.

Methods in combination: Creating a Symphony of Insights

When you combine different methods something 'magical' takes place. Instead of treating fundamental, technical, and sentiment analysis as separate, smart investors blend them. This creates a symphony of insights, making their decisions more reliable.

Validation via Diversification: Strengthening Your Strategy

Think of it like this. Treat fundamental analysis as the foundation, technical analysis as the framework, and sentiment analysis as the colour palette of your investment strategy. Each approach brings something unique, creating a strong decision-making framework that can handle the unpredictable market.

Analysing the market is about using a combo of fundamental, technical, and sentiment analysis. It's not about picking one over the other. It is understanding the strengths of each and together taking a complete view of the market.

As you explore market analysis, remember that successful investors blend. They rhyme analytics with sentiment. While you enjoy the complexity, let your market analysis be the compass guiding you through the financial terrain.

**Case Study:**

Analytical Harmony in Mumbai

Meet Raj, an avid trader from Mumbai, as we explore the diverse perspectives on markets discussed in Chapter 7.

Different Analytical Perspectives:

Raj engages with fundamental analysis, technical analysis, and sentiment analysis. Through his journey, readers discover how these distinct perspectives provide a comprehensive view of the financial markets.

Utilizing Tools for Market Analysis: Raj employs a range of tools, from technical indicators and economic calendars to sentiment gauging tools. By integrating these tools into his analytical framework, he gains a holistic understanding of market dynamics.

Reading the Collective Mind:

Raj delves into utilizing surveys and social media trends, effectively reading the collective mind of the market. This unique approach enhances his decision-making process, offering valuable insights into market sentiments.

Blending Analytical Methods:

Raj recognizes that each analytical type comes on a basis. He combines fundamental, technical, and sentiment analysis. This blending approach serves as the foundation, framework, and color palette for his investment strategy.

Key Takeaways for Traders in Mumbai: Crafting a Comprehensive Analytical Approach

Viewpoints matter: Raj's journey stresses the significance of looking at various analytical views to gain an understanding of the markets.

Tools of the Trade: The readers get exposed to practical tools such as technical indicators, economic calendars, and sentiment gauging tools, showcasing their relevance in market analysis.

Reading Market Sentiments: Raj realizes the value of being able to read the so called 'collective mind' of the market. It offers readers a strategic approach to understanding and responding to market sentiments.

Holistic Decision Validation: Raj showcases the value of combining various analytical techniques, including fundamental, technical, and sentiment analysis. He validates trading decisions in a holistic manner. Hence this offers valuable insights for the traders (in Mumbai!) looking for a thorough strategy for evaluating the market.

Key Points:

1. Different perspectives on markets: fundamental analysis, technical analysis, and sentiment analysis.

2. Tools for market analysis: technical indicators, economic calendars, and sentiment gauging tools.

3. Reading the collective mind: utilizing surveys and social media trends.

4. Combining analytical methods: blending fundamental, technical, and sentiment analysis for a comprehensive view.

5. Diverse approaches for decision validation; treating fundamental, technical and sentiment analysis as the foundation framework and color pallete of investment strategy.

# Chapter 8

# Investment Strategies: Tailored for Your Financial Journey?

*"There is a time to go long, a time to go short and a time to go fishing."* – Jesse Livermore

Whether are not you look at the long or short of it we want our money to work for us. This is like choosing the ultimate ride for your financial adventure.

Let me break down the two main strategies-long-term investing and short-term trading. We will figure out how to match them with your goals and comfort level.

Long-Term Investing: Growing Resilient Trees

Long-term investing mimics nature. It is like planting seeds and watching them grow into strong trees. It's about holding onto your investments and then, for some time, forgetting about it. Wait till the benefit from compounding returns - that slow and steady growth of your money which we all long for.

Short-Term Trading: Braving the Waves

Short-term trading is when you sail the waves. This is all about quick gains- buying and selling frequently. It's for the fast-paced  -an approach that needs a sharp eye on market trends, quick decision-making and excellent execution.

Pros and Cons: Weighing the Balance

Long-Term Investing: Patience Pays Off

More often than not, long-term investing gives larger compounded goodies. But, be ready for the downside - it takes patience as returns might take time, and you'll have to handle market ups and downs.

Short-Term Trading: Quick Gains, Quick Risks

Short-term trading is all about agility and quick gains. Risks are higher and so are the stress and the transaction costs. You need to have a certain mindset (innate) to tolerate risk at a such a consistent scale. Traders here stay alert, ready to adapt swiftly to market changes.

Choosing Your Financial Vessel: Aligning Strategies with Your Goals

Aligning Strategies with Personal Objectives: Your Financial Compass:

Long-term investors go for goals like retirement or wealth accumulation, matching well with their patient approach. Short-term traders might want a quick income or take advantage of specific market conditions. Your goals guide your strategy.

Risk Tolerance: When Riding the Waves

In a nutshell, this is your emotional and financial capacity to handle volatility-the downs with the ups. Long-term investors usually have higher risk tolerance. Short-term traders need lower risk tolerance as they navigate rapid market shifts.

Your Finanacial Journey: Your Personal Voyage

Your journey with your finances over a lifetime is like crossing an ocean. Your choice between a majestic cruise ship (long-term investing) or a nimble sailboat (short-term trading) should match your desired destination and comfort with unpredictability.

As you prepare to embark on your financial journey, consider your financial aspirations and risk tolerance. Do you desire a steady and stable path towards wealth accumulation, or are you willing to take on risk and navigate unpredictable waters for the chance at swifter gains? There is no universally correct answer, as your financial voyage is tailored to your individual preferences and goals. By familiarizing yourself with both approaches, you can select the strategy that aligns with your financial style and set sail towards a fulfilling and rewarding journey. Choose your financial vessel wisely and may your journey be as rewarding as the destination that awaits you!

**Case Study:**

Navigating Waves in Chennai – Long-Term vs. Short-Term Strategies

Meet Ananya, an aspiring trader from Chennai, as we delve into the contrasting strategies discussed in Chapter 8.

Long-Term Investing: Ananya, with a long-term perspective, envisions her investments as seeds planted for slow, steady growth. Exploring concepts from the chapter, readers follow Ananya's journey as she strategically selects assets aligned with her retirement goals.

Short-Term Trading: Switching gears, Ananya explores short-term trading, likening it to sailing waves for quick gains. This part of the case study emphasizes the need for a sharp eye, quick decisions, and adaptability to the fast-paced nature of short-term trading.

Strategic Goal Alignment:

The case study compares the benefits and risks of long-term investing for steady growth against the quick gains and higher risks associated with short-term trading. Ananya's experiences serve as a practical guide for readers in Chennai aiming to align strategies with their unique financial goals.

Key Takeaways for Traders in Chennai:

Tailoring Strategies to Goals, Planting Seeds for the Future: Ananya's long-term investing approach emphasizes the importance of patience, allowing investments to grow steadily over time.

Sailing Waves for Quick Gains: The short-term trading segment introduces readers to the energetic world of quick gains, encouraging them to hone their decision-making skills for this dynamic environment.

Match Strategies with Goals: Ananya's journey highlights the critical need to align trading strategies with individual financial goals. Readers in Chennai gain insights into tailoring approaches for a rewarding financial journey.

Key Points:

1. Long term or quick wins, let your money work. I'll explain long-term investing and short-term trading to suit your goals.

2. Like planting seeds, hold onto investments for slow, steady growth.

3. Sail waves, aim for quick gains through frequent buying and selling. Fast-paced, needs a sharp eye, and quick decisions.

4. Long-term investing brings steady growth with ups and downs. Short-term trading offers quick gains but has higher risks, stress, and costs.

5. Long-term for retirement, short-term for quick income. Consider risk tolerance - higher for long-term, lower for short-term. Your financial journey is unique, so choose wisely for a rewarding

# Chapter 9

# Taming Market Waves: Is Resilience the Key?

*"If most traders would learn to sit on their hands 50 percent of the time, they would make a lot more money." - Bill Lipschutz*

More often than not, the market is like a wild sea with lots of ups and downs! So, in this chapter, we'll chat about staying strong when the market gets wild. It's not just about numbers; it's also about having a tough mindset.

Building Mental Resilience in Turbulent Markets:

Recognizing Market Volatility: Markets have their highs and lows, just like the sea has waves. Think of your mind as a ship sailing these financial waters. To keep it steady, accept that market ups and downs are normal. Just accept it and move on.

Staying Calm with Practical Techniques: Let's delve into pragmatic methods for staying composed amidst market turbulence. Adopt a long-term perspective, akin to navigating a ship toward a distant island. While individual market waves may seem significant, they're merely transient disturbances on your overarching journey. Activities like meditation or a leisurely walk serve as stabilizing anchors during the storm, particularly when you've already embraced a long-term outlook.

For short-term traders, these fluctuations are precisely why you've entered into short-term positions-to capitalize on volatility, extract valuable lessons, and methodically handle risk and account management.

Understanding Market Cycles and Their Impact on Resilience:

a. Knowing Investor Sentiments: Markets move through cycles that affect how people feel about investing. It's like checking the weather at sea to be ready for storms and enjoy good times.

b. Adapting Strategies to Market Phases: Resilient investors adjust their strategies based on what's happening. When things are good, they focus on making money. In tough times, they protect what they have. Being resilient means going with the market flow, not fighting it.

In the ever-changing finance world, being tough is like dropping an anchor in stormy waters. By understanding that market ups and downs are normal, taking a long-term view, managing stress, adapting to market cycles, and adjusting strategies, you make your mental ship strong. Being tough is not just a trait; it's a skill you can get better at. Just like a ship gets stronger with each storm, you become more resilient with each market challenge. Learn the art of resilience, and you won't just survive the storms - you'll use their energy for a better journey. As long as you effectively handle your capital, preserve your funds, and avoid risking everything, each passing phase will contribute to your growing strength.

**Case Study:**

Resilience on the Mumbai Stock Exchange

Meet Arjun, an experienced trader from Mumbai, as we explore the concepts of resilience in Chapter 9.

Embracing Market Fluctuations:

Arjun compares the financial market to the turbulent seas surrounding Mumbai. Readers follow his journey as he navigates the ups and downs, viewing market fluctuations as a normal part of the trading expedition.

Tough Mindset and Long-Term Perspective:

Arjun adopts a tough mindset, accepting market challenges as opportunities for personal growth. The case study emphasizes the benefits of a long-term perspective and activities like meditation to stay composed during turbulent times.

Strategic Resilience:

Arjun's understanding of market cycles and strategic resilience becomes a guide for readers in Mumbai. Whether it's capitalizing on volatility as a short-term trader or preserving funds as a long-term investor, Arjun's experiences offer practical insights.

Key Takeaways for Traders in Mumbai: Building Resilience Amidst Market Storms

Embrace Market Fluctuations: Arjun's perspective encourages traders in Mumbai to accept market fluctuations, viewing them as a normal part of the trading journey.

Tough Mindset for Tough Markets: Adopting a tough mindset allows traders to navigate the financial waters with composure, fostering personal and financial growth.

Strategic Resilience: Arjun's strategies for understanding market cycles and adjusting approaches contribute to Mumbai traders' resilience. Effective capital management, preserving funds, and avoiding excessive risk emerge as crucial elements in the journey.

Key Points:

1. Picture the market as a wild sea, full of ups and downs. Explore how to stay strong amidst the chaos.

2. Embrace a tough mindset to navigate the financial waters. Accept market fluctuations as a normal part of the journey and move forward.

3. Adopt a long-term perspective and use activities like meditation to stay composed during market turbulence. Short-term traders can capitalize on volatility and manage risk strategically.

4. Understand market cycles and adjust your strategies accordingly. Resilience means going with the market flow, whether it's time to make money or protect what you have.

5. Like a ship strengthening in storms, developing resilience through market challenges contributes to personal growth. Effective capital management, preserving funds, and avoiding excessive risk are key elements in this journey.

Finding value in your journey towards financial success with this book? Your positive reviews can inspire and guide fellow traders on their path to success. Share your insights and experiences, helping others discover the transformative impact of 'Trade Smart'. Your review isn't just feedback—it's a beacon illuminating the way for others. Thank you for being part of this empowering community.

# Chapter 10

# Mindfulness in Trading: Calmness as Strategy?

*"If you can learn to create a state of mind that is not affected by the market's behavior, the struggle will cease to exist." –Mark Douglas*

Diving into the realm of trading with poise and intelligence is what we aim for in this section. Here, the spotlight is on how mindfulness can significantly boost your trading performance on a day-to-day basis.

The Incredible Benefits of Mindfulness in Trading:

Enhanced Concentration for Superior Decisions:

Mindfulness is the practice of being fully engaged in the present moment. For traders, this can lead to improved focus during decision-making, minimized distractions, and the ability to more accurately assess the market for well-informed choices.

Reduced Stress for Clearer Thinking:

Indeed, the markets can be a source of stress and anxiety. Fortunately, mindfulness has been shown to decrease stress levels, fostering a balanced state of mind essential for tackling the challenges of trading. A serene mind is more adept at handling market volatility without hasty reactions.

Integrating Mindfulness into Your Trading Routine:

Brief Pauses for Mental Rejuvenation:

In the swift-paced trading environment, short instances of mindfulness can act as mental refreshments. A few minutes devoted to mindfulness exercises can instill a sense of peace and clarity, refreshing your strategy outlook. There's a wealth of mindfulness techniques available online, many at no cost. Find one that resonates with you and make it a part of your daily practice for maximum benefit.

Pre-Trading Mindfulness Warm-up:

Mindfulness exercises prior to trading sessions prime your mental state, akin to honing your instruments. A brief breathing routine can aid in centering your focus, shutting out extraneous disturbances, and preparing you to enter the market with a tranquil mindset.

Total Engagement in Trading Activities:

Traders who embrace mindfulness are completely absorbed in their tasks, allowing for swift adaptation to market changes, strategic adjustments, and informed decision-making as events unfold.

Elevating Focus and Decision-Making through Mindfulness:

Staying Vigilant for Wise Decisions:

The essence of sound trading decisions lies in being fully attentive. Mindful traders are better at processing information, analyzing trends with precision, and conducting trades confidently. Being vigilant and tuned into the market is a critical ability enhanced by mindfulness.

Eliminating Distractions for Considerate Choices:

Distractions can undermine effective trading. Mindfulness serves as a barrier against such interruptions, enabling traders to concentrate on the essential elements. By diminishing external clutter, traders are poised to make considerate decisions that align with their strategies, steering clear of rash, externally driven actions.

Adopting mindfulness in trading transcends a mere trend; it revolutionizes traders' approach, infusing trading with serenity, focus, and resilience. Mindfulness injects a human touch into the numeric and chart-dominated trading world, fostering decision-making prowess and a balanced, sustainable method for navigating financial markets. As you venture into trading, reflect on the profound effects mindfulness can have on both your success and overall quality of life in this dynamic domain.

Mindfulness Practices:

Daily Mindfulness Habit

Consistent mindfulness practice hones your focus and alleviates stress, thus equipping you to tackle trading with a lucid mind. Here's a straightforward, 5-minute daily mindfulness routine designed for traders:

Step 1: Seek a Peaceful Spot

Commence by finding a tranquil and comfortable space for undisturbed sitting. This could be at your trading desk before market hours or a quiet corner at home.

Step 2: Breath Focus

With a relaxed sitting posture and eyes closed, inhale deeply through your nose, filling your lungs fully. Exhale slowly through your mouth. Continue this deep breathing for about a minute, concentrating solely on the act of breathing.

Step 3: Body Scan

After establishing a steady breath rhythm, shift your focus to the top of your head, progressively moving your attention down through your body. Observe any sensations, tightness, or discomfort without trying to change them. This mindful body scan should take around two minutes.

Step 4: Thoughts Acknowledgment

As thoughts surface, recognize them without judgement and let them drift away. Envision your thoughts as leaves floating on a stream, coming and going. This practice helps foster a state of mind where market ups and downs don't disturb your inner calm.

Step 5: Intentions Setting

In the concluding minute, set your intentions for the trading day ahead. Aim to remain present, base your decisions on analysis rather than emotion, and keep your cool amidst market movements.

Mindful Trading Meditation

The script below is meant for a mindful trading meditation. Consider recording your voice reading it for playback, or simply follow it as you read:

Start with Finding Your Breath

Sit with a straight back and hands on your lap, comfortably. Close your eyes and take a deep breath in. Pause briefly, then exhale slowly. Let your breathing settle into a natural rhythm.

Ground Yourself

Feel your body's weight against the chair and your feet's contact with the ground. Anchor yourself in the present.

Observe Without Judgment

It's natural for thoughts of past trades, market trends, or future worries to emerge as you meditate. Watch these thoughts without attaching any judgment. They are neither positive nor negative; they just exist.

Return to Your Breath

Whenever your mind wanders, gently redirect your attention back to your breath. Feel the air entering and leaving your body. This is your anchor.

Visualize Calm Decision-Making

Picture yourself reviewing the markets, observing price fluctuations. In this vision, you're at peace, making choices based on logic and strategy. You're completely engaged, not dwelling on past losses or fearing future setbacks.

Embrace a Mindful Trading Day

As the meditation concludes, take several deep breaths, imagining each inhale brings confidence and calmness, and each exhale releases any lingering tension. Open your eyes when ready, taking this mindfulness into your trading day.

By incorporating these mindfulness exercises into your daily regimen, you create a mental space conducive to focused, tranquil, and strategic trading. Remember, mindfulness is a skill that improves with practice. Over time, you'll see these practices not only boost your trading performance but also enhance your general well-being.

Case Study:

The Essence of Mindfulness in Delhi Trading

Explore Neha's story, a devoted Delhi trader, in Chapter 10 as we unravel the importance of mindfulness in trading.

Staying Focused Amid Chaos:

Neha's trading journey underscores the value of focus. The case study shows how taking brief pauses and engaging in pre-trading exercises aid in maintaining clarity amidst market turmoil.

Mindfully Adapting Strategies:

Neha's proactive, responsive trading method serves as an example for Delhi traders. The case study highlights how mindfulness supports confident decision-making and the adjustment of strategies with a human-centric approach.

Essential Insights from Neha: Achieving Mindfulness in Trading

Maintain Focus: Neha's tale urges us to remain attentive, lessen stress, and make wiser choices in the volatile markets.

Active and Adaptable: Neha's dynamic trading style, enriched by mindfulness, acts as a guide for Delhi traders to mindfully modify strategies, improving decision-making.

A Sustainable, People-oriented Method: The case study celebrates Neha's adoption of a sustainable, people-focused strategy for a better trading journey. Traders in Delhi can learn the significance of melding decision-making with mindfulness for a balanced approach.

Key Insights:

1. Keep focused, reduce stress, and make smarter choices.

2. Embrace brief pauses and pre-trading routines for clear thinking.

3. Stay dynamic, swiftly respond, and adjust strategies with mindfulness.

4. Remain vigilant, assimilate information, and make confident selections while sidestepping distractions.

5. Adopt a sustainable, people-focused strategy for enhanced decision-making and a harmonious trading experience.

# Chapter 11

# Patience & Consistency: Trading's Winning Duo? - Part I

*"Why do you think unsuccessful traders are obsessed with market analysis? They crave the sense of certainty that analysis appears to give them. Although few would admit it, the truth is that the typical trader wants to be right on every single trade. He is desperately trying to create certainty where it just doesn't exist."* –Mark Douglas

Patience and consistency are like having superpowers for traders. Let's break down why waiting for the right opportunities and staying consistent are crucial for long-term success in trading.

Why Patience Matters:

In trading, the urge for quick profits often leads to bad decisions. But savvy traders know that real success comes from patience - waiting for the right opportunities. Understanding that the best opportunities take time sets successful traders apart. Whether you are timing the market short term or long term it is still a mind-game - your perception of time at that moment will impact your decisions and action. So, keep a strong objective reign on your perception management. It can be easily achieved with the help of a check list and rule-based approach (just like I mention above).

Patience isn't just twiddling your thumbs; it means getting how the market works. By embracing patience, traders avoid rushed or badly timed trades. This not only keeps their money safe but also positions them strategically for the long run.

# Chapter 12

# Patience & Consistency: Trading's Winning Duo? -Part II

Building Consistent Habits: A Blueprint for Trading Success

Consistency is key in trading. It's not about luck; it's about creating routines and strategies that give you reliable results over time. Successful traders stick to good habits, not random bursts of brilliance.

Think of it like a recipe for Skill Building stated by the following equation:

## P+ER+FL+H = ESB

Meaning...
(Protocol + Effective Routines + Feedback Loops + Habituation = Effective Skill Building).

Here's how it breaks down:

Establishing Habits: The 60 to 90 Days Rule
In 1960, Dr. Maxwell Maltz proposed that it takes 21 days to instill a habit. However, for a strong trading habit, consistent effort over 60 to 90 days is recommended. This prolonged commitment ensures the habit becomes deeply ingrained in your trading routine.

Protocol: Follow Steps in Order

Imagine a recipe - you follow the steps one by one. In trading, having a clear plan (protocol) helps guide your decisions and keeps things organized.

Effective Routines:

Prioritize Your Actions
Just like getting ready in the morning, you have routines. Make your trading routines efficient and in line with your plan.

## Feedback Loops: Learn from Mistakes

Think of feedback loops like checking your reflection in the mirror. Regularly measure, verify, and learn from your mistakes to get better.

## Habituation: Make Things a Habit

Habituation is turning actions into habits. Repeat your routines until they become second nature, like brushing your teeth every day.

## Creating Support Mechanisms: Identifying Your Routine:

Identifying a routine becomes your support mechanism. Consider starting your day with exercise, a brief 10 to 20 minutes of calisthenics and stretching to energize your system. Hydrate with a large glass of water, fuelling your body for optimal mental function. A light, nutritious breakfast and reviewing your Plan and Trading Rules are vital components of your routine.

## Building Skill Levels:

Combine all these elements, and you're building skills. It's not about being a genius; it's about consistently doing the right things.

## Why Consistency Matters?

Disciplined habits are crucial for establishing a dependable trading methodology. By adhering to tried-and-true strategies, continually assessing the market landscape, and executing trades in a systematic manner, traders can achieve consistent success over time. This approach, combined with the P+ER+FL+H framework, forms a robust foundation for generating profits, enabling traders to navigate market fluctuations with confidence and adaptability.

## Mechanical and Internal Data: The Daily Trading Strategy:

Review your daily trading strategy out loud. This practice flushes out distortions, providing clarity and strengthening your confidence. Routines like this address both your "mechanical data" and your "internal data."

By incorporating these routines into your daily practice, you not only automate your trading but also cultivate the patience and consistency required for long-term success in the dynamic world of financial markets.

Now, it's like having a clear recipe for success in trading. Stick with it, and you'll see the results over time!

## Balancing Action and Patience:

Trading is like a mix of jumping in at the right time and waiting patiently. You've got to be quick to grab good chances when they come up, but also chill during times when the market's all over the place. The best traders get this balance right. They know not every moment is perfect for making a move, so they wait it out when they need to.

Finding the best times to trade is about being ready, having a solid plan, and waiting for the market to show you the green light. The traders who really do well are the ones who nail this mix. They make moves that are thought-out and happen at just the right time, which helps them win big in the long run.

Being patient and consistent is super important in trading. Patience means you can wait for the perfect shot instead of jumping the gun and possibly losing money. Being consistent helps you build a strong trading game that can withstand the ups and downs of the market. Getting the hang of both doing stuff and waiting is key to making it big in the trading world. By sticking to these ideas, traders can do well over time and handle whatever the market throws at them.

The Power of Patience in Wall Street Trading

Meet Emily, a seasoned trader on Wall Street, as we explore the key takeaways from Chapter 11.

Avoiding Impulsive Decisions:

Emily's success story revolves around embracing patience—a crucial aspect discussed in Chapter 11. The case study showcases how Emily's ability to wait for the right opportunities has been the cornerstone of her success.

Establishing Reliable Trading Habits:

Emily's daily routines, kickstarted with exercise, hydration, and plan reviews, exemplify the essential support mechanisms discussed in Chapter 11. Her disciplined approach provides valuable insights for traders aiming to establish reliable habits.

Prioritize Actions:

Emily's success is a testament to the importance of prioritizing actions and learning from mistakes. Traders on Wall Street can benefit from her approach to skill development over 60-90 days.

Balance Action and Patience:

Emily's story emphasizes the need to balance action and patience. Traders can learn to be prepared, have a clear strategy, and patiently wait for ideal market conditions—leading to long-term success in the financial markets.

Key Points:

1. Embracing patience by avoiding impulsive decisions-the key to success lies in waiting for the right opportunities and managing your perception of time.

2. Over 60-90 days, develop a trading habit by following a plan, prioritizing actions, learning from mistakes, and turning routines into second nature.

3. Take hold of your daily routines. Like kick-start your day with exercise, hydrate, and review your plans - essential support mechanisms that pave the way for trading success.

4. To become successful in trading, you go to focus on consistent efforts: follow a plan, prioritize actions, learn from mistakes, and turn them into daily habits for skill development.

5. Balance action and patience in your trading journey. Be prepared, have a clear strategy, and patiently wait for ideal market conditions - the recipe for long-term success in the financial markets.

# Chapter 13

# Why Are Trading Journals Magical?

*"Do more of what works and less of what doesn't."* – *Steve Clark*

Making money isn't just luck-it's a skill you can learn. Let's delve into something crucial: your Trading Journal.

Think of it as your map through the crazy market journey. It's not just about noting trades; it's like creating a roadmap for your trading adventure.

Your trading journal is like a history book of your trades. It's not just a rule to write down when you enter and exit; it's a strategy. Jotting down why you made each trade sets you up for learning and improvement.

Now, your journal is not just a boring ledger; it's a live tracker. Numbers and trends on its pages give you a clear picture of your wins and losses. It's like having a weather forecast for your trading strategies - helping you navigate unpredictable market terrain.

Here are 3 Essential Pillars to building a Trading Foundation:

Specialized Education: Understanding the intricacies of the financial markets is paramount. Specialized education equips traders with the knowledge needed to navigate the complexities of trading.

Skill Development: Building and honing trading skills is an ongoing process. Skill development ensures that traders stay adaptive and proficient in their decision-making processes. Like for example my advice to student is always this:

"IMPORTANT! You should never trade real money until you have proven your ability to be profitable on a simulated account!

I promise, if you can't make money on a simulated account, you won't do it on a live account.
Don't start trading a live account until you've proven you have acquired the necessary skills to make money on a practice account."

Self-Discipline: The ability to adhere to a set of rules and maintain composure under various market conditions is a hallmark of successful traders. Self-discipline is the glue that holds the other pillars together.

You can get a sample of a typical trading journal in the index/ exhibit pages.

Beyond the numbers, your trading journal is your personal teacher. It's waiting for you to find lessons in its pages. Looking back at your trades shows patterns in your decisions. What worked great, and where did you mess up? Knowing your strengths and weaknesses is the first step to getting better.

Your journal is a goldmine of data. Analyse past trades not just for outcomes but for the journey. Understand the ins and outs of your decision-making process. This self-reflection is the key to improving your strategies.

Like in any form of personal development, improvement is a must for a trader. Lessons from your journal pave the way for getting better. Adapting your strategies based on past experiences isn't admitting failure; it's showing you can change - just like successful traders do.

A trader's journey is always changing. Each entry in your journal takes you a step closer to mastering the game. It's not about doing something entirely new each time; it's about making small adjustments, improving your decision-making, and getting mentally stronger.

In conclusion, a detailed trading journal isn't just for keeping records; it's your personalized success guide. It's the compass navigating you through the tricky seas of financial markets. Your journal is more than a ledger; it's a mentor, a friend, and a roadmap to lasting success. Embrace the art of journaling, and you'll see that success, once hard to catch, is now within your reach.

**Case Study:**

The Trading Journal Journey of Sarah

Meet Sarah, a passionate trader in the bustling financial district of New York, as we delve into the key concepts from Chapter 12.

Trading Journal as Your Map: Sarah understands that a trading journal is not just about noting trades; it's her roadmap through the unpredictable market journey. Her commitment to maintaining a detailed journal serves as a guiding light in her trading endeavours.

Essential Pillars for Trading Foundation: Sarah's success is attributed to the foundational elements discussed in Chapter 12:

a. Specialized Education: Sarah continuously enhances her understanding of financial markets.

b. Skill Development: Actively engaged in an ongoing process to stay adaptive and proficient.

c. Self-Discipline: Sarah adheres to rules, maintaining composure under various market conditions.

Key Takeaways for Traders: Building a Solid Foundation

Continuous Learning: Sarah's dedication to ongoing education emphasizes the significance of staying informed in the ever-evolving financial landscape.

Discipline and Rule Adherence: Traders can learn from Sarah's commitment to discipline, using it as a tool to navigate the complexities of the market.

The Power of the Trading Journal: Sarah's trading journal is not just a record; it's a teacher, revealing patterns, strengths, weaknesses, and acting as a goldmine of data for constant improvement.

Sarah's Journal: A Path to Improvement

Sarah's journey serves as inspiration for traders aiming to build a solid foundation, emphasizing the transformative power of a well-maintained trading journal.

Key Points:

1. Trading Journal is Your Map: Not just about noting trades; it's your roadmap through the unpredictable market journey, helping you learn and improve.

2. Essential Pillars for Trading Foundation:

a. Specialized Education: Understanding financial markets is crucial.

b. Skill Development: Ongoing process to stay adaptive and proficient.

c. Self-Discipline: Adhering to rules and maintaining composure under various market conditions.

3. Thirteen Best Trading Practices:

a. Proper education and continuous learning.

b. Excellent discipline.

c. Understanding and calculating risks in advance.

d. Always using stops.

e. Avoiding revenge trading and overtrading.

f. Not trading compulsively or letting emotions guide trades.

g. Having a detailed plan, a proven strategy, and being connected to a community.

4. Beyond numbers, your trading journal is a personal teacher waiting for you to find lessons in its pages. It reveals patterns in your decisions, strengths, weaknesses, and is a goldmine of data.

5. Lessons from your journal pave the way for improvement. Adapting strategies based on past experiences is a

sign of change, just like successful traders do. Your trading journey is about making small adjustments, improving decision-making, and getting mentally stronger for lasting success.

# Chapter 14

# Resilience in Trading: Turning Losses Into Wins?

*"Confidence is not 'I will profit on this trade.' Confidence is 'I will be fine if I don't profit from this trade." – Yvan Byeajee*

We will create a survival guide for you here dealing with the stress that come with losses. Let's dive into some strategies that will not only help you bounce back emotionally but also set the stage for future success.

Facing Losses: They're Not the End

Yep, losses happen in trading. It's not about dodging them; it's about seeing them as steps toward getting better. First off, accept that, and you're on your way to being emotionally tough.

Avoiding Emotional Trades After a Loss: Stay Cool
When you lose, emotions can mess with your decisions. Fear and frustration might make you do impulsive stuff. It's super important to take a step back, rethink your strategies, and resist making hasty decisions. Keep your cool. It is the key to getting back in control.

Learning from Mistakes: Turn Setbacks into Lessons

Behind every mess-up, there are lessons waiting to be found. Good traders don't see losses as dead ends but as chances to learn. Try to figure out what went wrong. By checking out bad trades, you can find patterns, see weaknesses, and make your strategies stronger.

Taking Action: Make Changes for Success

Learning from losses is great, but it's even better when you do something about it. This could mean changing how you handle risks, adjusting when you jump in or out of trades, or mixing up your investments. Taking action is the only way for turning screw-ups into chances for positive change.

Staying Positive:
Mind Over Matter

Keeping a positive mindset is crucial. Focus on what you've learned instead of just thinking about losses. Seeing screw-ups as chances to grow helps you stay positive. This shift doesn't just make you feel better; it helps you handle future challenges better too.

Building Resilience:

Resilience is like the backbone of successful trading. Instead of letting draw-downs crush your confidence, use them as stepping stones for growth.

This chapter is your guide to handling draw-downs. Embrace losses, sidestep emotional traps, learn from mistakes, take decisive action, stay positive, and build resilience. In trading, mistakes are stepping stones to growth and success in the dynamic world of finance.

Embracing Losses – Mark's Journey to Growth

Meet Mark, an experienced trader who navigates the unpredictable market landscape with resilience and a positive mindset, as we explore the key concepts from Chapter 13.

Embrace Losses for Growth: Mark understands that losses are an inherent part of trading and views them as opportunities for improvement. His approach to losses is a testament to his commitment to personal and professional growth.

Maintain Emotional Control: Mark remains calm and composed after facing losses. Instead of succumbing to impulsive decisions driven by emotions, he takes a rational approach to regain control. He vsualizes a positive outcome and becomes mindful of his thoughts.

Learn from Setbacks: Rather than seeing losses as setbacks, Mark treats them as valuable lessons. He analyses patterns, identifies weaknesses, and strengthens his trading strategies based on the insights gained.

Act on Insights: Mark doesn't just reflect on losses; he takes proactive steps to modify his approach. His ability to translate insights into positive changes contributes to his continuous improvement.

Stay Positive, Build Resilience:
Mark focuses on growth, not dwelling on losses. This positive mindset helps him build resilience, an essential trait for navigating the dynamic and challenging nature of financial markets.

Key Takeaways for Traders:
Transforming Losses into Opportunities

Embracing Losses: Mark's journey illustrates the importance of accepting losses as opportunities for improvement and growth.

Emotional Control: Traders can learn from Mark's approach to maintaining emotional control, avoiding impulsive decisions during challenging times.

Learning from Setbacks: Mark's proactive approach to learning from setbacks emphasizes the value of treating losses as lessons for strategy refinement.

Building Resilience: Mark's positive mindset and focus on growth contribute to his resilience, a crucial element for long-term success in trading.

Mark's story serves as a source of inspiration for traders, showcasing the transformative power of embracing losses as part of the journey to becoming a successful trader.

Key Points:

1. In order to grow you have to accept reasonable losses: Accept losses as part of trading and opportunities to improve.

2. Stay in control of your Emotions: Stay calm post-loss to avoid impulsive decisions and regain control.

3. Setbacks are good teachers: Treat losses as lessons to identify patterns and strengthen strategies.

4. When you get an insight act on it: Modify your approach based on what you learn from losses for positive change.

5. In trading it is essential to have a positive mindset while building youre resilience muscles: Focus on growth,

not losses, to maintain a positive mindset and develop resilience.

Enjoying your journey towards financial success with this book? Your positive feedback can help others too! Share your thoughts and experiences, and inspire fellow traders. Your review isn't just a review—it's a helpful guide for others. Thanks for being part of our community.

# Chapter 15

# Mastering Emotions: What's the Secret?

*"Markets can remain irrational longer than you can remain solvent." –John Maynard Keynes*

Over and above the Charts, your feelings and emotions play a key role. Because these emotions mess with your trades. Psychological management is the first step to managing risk. Fear makes you pause, worried about losses, while greed pushes for more profits, sometimes leading to risky moves.

Understanding Fear and Greed:
The Dynamic Duo

Fear is like hitting pause, making you hesitate about potential losses. On the flip side, greed promises more profits, tempting risky decisions. They mess with your plans, making you panic, sell, or take unnecessary risks.

Realizing Their Impact: Navigating Emotions

Understanding how fear and greed mess with your decisions is crucial. They can mess up your plans, but don't worry! Knowing these emotions is the first step to a smart trading approach.

Managing Emotional Extremes:
Rules and Rational Analysis

Now, let's talk about practical techniques. Think of them as your compass during stormy market weather.

Rule 1: Define Your Risk Tolerance
Decide how much risk you can handle beforehand. This way, fear won't push you into reckless decisions.

Rule 2: Stick to Your Trading Plan
Create a solid plan and stick to it. This shields you from greedy impulses, keeping you on track.

Rule 3: Use Stop-Loss Orders
Set automated orders to limit losses and counteract fear's impact. This helps you stay in control during market downturns.

Balancing Act:

Emotions vs. Logic

Balancing emotions with logic is key. Try these strategies:

Strategy 1: Practice Mindfulness

Stay present with mindfulness techniques. This helps you make rational decisions despite fear and greed.

Strategy 2: Review and Adjust Strategies

Keep improving! Analyze past trades to refine your strategies and adapt to market changes.

Strategy 3: Seek External Perspectives

Connect with mentors or trading communities for diverse insights. This helps you decide beyond fear and greed.

Case Study: Fear and Greed Management – Sarah's Strategic Approach

Meet Sarah, an astute trader who effectively manages the impact of fear and greed on her decision-making, reflecting the key concepts discussed in Chapter 14.

Emotions Affecting Decisions: Sarah acknowledges the significant influence of fear and greed on trading decisions. Understanding this, she actively seeks strategies to mitigate their disruptive effects.

Managing Fear and Greed: Sarah uses well-defined rules to handle fear and greed. By setting clear risk tolerance levels, sticking to her trading plan, and implementing stop-loss orders, she maintains control over her emotions during market volatility.

Balancing Emotions and Logic: To achieve a balance between emotions and logic, Sarah employs mindfulness techniques. Regularly practicing mindfulness helps her stay focused, make rational decisions, and avoid succumbing to emotional impulses.

Learning from Past Trades:
Sarah analyses her past trades systematically. This retrospective approach allows her to refine her strategies, identify patterns related to fear and greed, and continuously improve her decision-making process.

Seeking Diverse Insights: Recognizing the importance of diverse perspectives, Sarah actively seeks insights from mentors and trading communities. By doing so, she gains valuable perspectives beyond the influence of fear and greed, enhancing her overall trading strategy.

Key Takeaways for Traders: Navigating Emotional Challenges

Recognizing Emotional Impact:
Sarah's case emphasizes the need to acknowledge the influence of fear and greed on trading decisions.

Strategic Management: Sarah's approach involves implementing strategic measures, such as risk tolerance setting, adherence to a trading plan, and mindfulness to manage emotions effectively.

Continuous Improvement:

By learning from past trades and seeking diverse insights, Sarah underscores the importance of continuous improvement in navigating emotional challenges.

Balancing Emotions:

The case highlights the significance of balancing emotions and logic to make informed and rational decisions in the dynamic world of financial markets.

Sarah's story serves as a practical guide for traders, illustrating effective strategies to manage emotions and make informed decisions in the face of fear and greed.

Key Points:

1. Your emotions, like fear and greed, will affect trading decisions. This may cause you to hesitate and make risky moves.

2. You have to understand how fear and greed disrupt decisions. This will help you make smarter trading choices.

3. Use rules like defining risk tolerance, sticking to a plan, and employing stop-loss orders to manage emotions during market volatility.

4. Practices like "Mindfulness" will help you achieve a balance between emotion and logic while gauging externalities.

5. For refining strategies, analyze past trade data. Look for diverse insights from mentors or trading communities beyond the influence of fear and greed.

# Chapter 16

# Staying Sharp: Can Continuous Learning Propel Market Success?

*"The game taught me the game. And it didn't spare me the rod while teaching." - Jesse Livermore*

Why is it super important to keep learning in the ever-changing world of financial markets. Ready? Let's get started.

Change is the Name of the Game:

Financial markets are always changing. It's like a game where the rules are always shifting. To do well, you got to know that things are always in motion.

So, learn to be in the game, not just watching from the sidelines. You got to Act!

Stay in the Loop with Trends and Tools:

Keeping up with what's hot and the latest tools is not just about surviving; it's about grabbing cool opportunities. Trends pop up, tools get cooler, and strategies change. Learn to love the changes, and they can be your roadmap to success.

Resources are Your Best Friends:

When you're diving into the sea of knowledge, you need some trustworthy guides. Books, online classes, webinars, and communities are like your best friends. Hang out with them for a richer learning experience.

From Book Smarts to Street Smarts:

Knowing stuff is cool, but it's even cooler when you use it. Take what you learn and use it in your trading. Each trade is like a step in your learning adventure, turning what you read into real action.

Keep it Fresh with Updated Info:

In the financial world, having the latest info is like having a secret weapon. Learning isn't just about getting new facts; it's about staying in the know and making your strategies even better.

Key Points:

1. Financial markets are like a dynamic game with ever-changing rules; actively engage and adapt to the constant motion for success.

2. Staying current with the latest trends and tools is not merely a survival tactic but a means to seize exciting opportunities.

3. In your quest for knowledge, consider books, online classes, webinars, and communities as your trustworthy companions.

4. Knowledge gains value when applied; utilize what you learn in your trading endeavours for practical, real-world action.

5. In the financial realm, having the latest information is akin to possessing a secret weapon; continuous learning is about staying well-informed and refining your strategies with the freshest insights available.

# Chapter 17

## The Art of Balancing: Work, Life, and Trading

*"The biggest risk is not taking a risk. In a world that's changing really quickly, the only strategy that is guaranteed to fail is not taking risks." - Mark Zuckerberg*

Frankly, I need to emphasize here that after everything I have said so far,-the idea of money is only what it is-an idea. Money is an outcome of competence which can be developed with focused practice and consistency; life is much bigger. It's also about enjoying life beyond numbers and charts, right? Let's explore how to balance work, life, and trading for lasting success and personal fulfilment.

First off, life is more than just market buzz. Don't miss out on the joy of relationships, hobbies, and downtime. Now, to balance things, set clear boundaries. Don't fall for the lure of the markets-it will always be there. Look at allocating specific hours for trading. Do not let trading take over your life. Never.

Efficient time management is key. Dedicate specific hours to trading for discipline and routine, enhancing both your trading effectiveness and personal time. Keep personal and professional spaces separate. Create a mental switch to transition smoothly between focused trading and relaxing personal activities. This preserves your mental well-being and prevents burnout.

Recognize your limits to avoid over-trading. Taking regular breaks is essential for both mental and physical health. As a trader, you should focus on getting adequate sleep, regular exercise, and relaxation. Taking good care of your health and wellness will automatically have a positive effect on your trading days.

In a nutshell, mastering the balance between trading and personal life is an ongoing process. This guide encourages you to embrace balance as a key element of a prosperous and fulfilling life in the finance world.

Key Points:

1. Don't let the market consume you; cherish relationships, hobbies, and downtime for overall happiness.

2. Establish specific trading hours to maintain a healthy work-life balance, preventing market demands from encroaching on personal time.

3. Dedicate designated hours to trading for discipline, routine, and a smooth transition between focused trading and personal activities.

4. Avoid overtrading, take breaks, and prioritize sleep and relaxation for sustained financial and mental health.

5. Embrace balance as a continuous journey, recognizing its significance for a prosperous and fulfilling life in the finance world.

# Chapter 18

## How Powerful Is Mentorship?

*"If I hadn't had mentors, I wouldn't be here today. I'm a product of great mentoring, great coaching. Coaches or mentors are very important. They could be anyone-your husband, other family members, or your boss." -Indra Nooyi*

If you're young, listen up - finding a mentor and being part of a supportive community is a game-changer. Even if you are an older adult -nothing changes - learning is a path. Even you can benefit immensely from a dedicated Mentor. Here is how Mentors can make a difference:

Getting Wisdom from Mentors:

Think of mentors as your experienced guides in the trading adventure. They've been through it all and can show you shortcuts to financial success.

Learning from the Pros:

Mentors share their wins and losses, helping you dodge common mistakes that could cost you. It's like learning from their victories and slip-ups to avoid messing up yourself.

Skipping the School of Hard Knocks:

Mentorship is like having a shield against potential mistakes. They give you a roadmap, so you don't have to figure everything out through expensive trial and error.

The Power of Community:

Trading isn't a solo game anymore. Joining a community is like tapping into a giant pool of knowledge and support. Make sure that the program you choose has a robust mentorship program including access to a Trader's community.

Growing Together:

Communities are full of different trading styles and strategies. Info flows freely, and you can learn from others' experiences.

Having Backup in Tough Times:

Trading can be a rollercoaster, and your community becomes a lifeline. Peers offer support, share stories, and keep you going during the rough patches.

Using Everyone's Smarts:

Embrace the collective knowledge within your group. Everyone has a unique perspective, and this diversity helps you see beyond your own point of view.

Smart Decision-Making:

Collective knowledge helps you make informed decisions. The group's combined experience is a powerful tool for understanding markets better.

Key Points:

1. Mentors serve as experienced guides in the trading journey, offering shortcuts to financial success based on their wealth of experience.

2. Gain insights from mentors who share their victories and mistakes, helping you avoid common pitfalls and navigate the market more effectively.

3. Mentorship acts as a shield, providing a roadmap that saves you from costly trial and error, accelerating your learning curve.

4. Joining a trading community is like tapping into a vast pool of knowledge and support. Look for programs with

robust mentorship and access to a thriving traders' community.

5. In trading communities, diverse styles and strategies abound. Learn from others' experiences, receive support during tough times, and embrace collective knowledge for smarter decision-making in the dynamic market.

# Chapter 19

# Easy Steps to Trading Success

*"Tell me, and I forget, teach me and I may remember, involve me, and I learn." –Benjamin Franklin*

Welcome to the final chapter of our deep dive into the world of trading psychology. We've covered emotions, decision-making, and resilience in trading and investing. As we wrap up this book, let's take a moment to think, apply what we've learned, and grow.

Recap of Key Strategies:

Let's quickly revisit the important strategies we've picked up. We chatted about feelings like fear, greed, and hope in the financial world. It's not just knowing them; it's about handling them well.

In decision-making, we learned how emotions can lead to impulsive actions, especially when we're scared or overly excited about making money. Now, you've got tools to make smart decisions by understanding how your feelings can influence them.

Why Psychological Strategies Matter in Trading/Investing:

Beyond the technical stuff like market analysis and risk management, we explored how crucial our mind is in trading. Your mind is like a trader's superpower, but it can also play tricks. Strengthening your mind is like building a solid base for successful trading and investing.

Just as an architect plans every detail of a building, as a trader, you should carefully integrate psychological strategies into your trading plans. It's like an invisible power that safeguards your finances, especially when things get tough.

Applying What You've Learned in Real Trading:

Knowing things in theory is a start, but now it's time to put that knowledge into action. Don't let this new understanding sit quietly; apply it. Think of it as turning your knowledge into skills through practice.

When you start real trading, remember experience is the best teacher. Be mindful when you trade, using the psychological strategies you've learned. Picture your trading journey like a canvas where theory meets reality, creating a picture of smart decisions and profits.

Making Strategies a Habit in Your Trading Routine:

To get really good at something, make it part of your routine. Picture learning to play a new instrument; at first, it's about learning individual notes and techniques. True mastery comes when those elements blend into a beautiful melody. The same goes for your trading strategies.

Make it a habit to use psychological strategies every time you trade. Develop a routine before trading that includes focusing on techniques and risk management. Let these strategies become second nature, like a natural part of your trading style.

Understanding Growth in Trading Is Always Happening:

As you finish this book, remember your trading journey isn't a road trip with a fixed destination. It's more like an ongoing adventure where you keep growing and learning. Trading is always changing, and so should your approach to the mental side of it.

Realize there will be tough times, successes, and exciting moments. Each experience is like a stroke on the canvas of your trading mind, adding to the masterpiece you're creating.

Keep Learning and Adapting to Become a Better Trader:

In the ever-changing world of finance, the only sure thing is change. To stay ahead, keep learning and adapting. Be open to learning from both successes and mistakes. Listen to experienced traders, pick up insights from market trends, and be ready to improve your strategies.

To wrap it up, don't see this book as an end but as a beginning. It's the start of a lifelong journey into the challenging yet rewarding world of trading and investing. With psychological strategies, practical skills, and the understanding that growth is ongoing, you're not just a trader; you're the architect of your financial future.

May your future trades be successful, your decisions wise, and your journey in trading a continually enriching experience. Happy trading!

Key Points:

1. Mentors serve as experienced guides in the trading journey, offering shortcuts to financial success based on their wealth of experience.

2. Gain insights from mentors who share their victories and mistakes, helping you avoid common pitfalls and navigate the market more effectively.

3. Mentorship acts as a shield, providing a roadmap that saves you from costly trial and error, accelerating your learning curve.

4. Joining a trading community is like tapping into a vast pool of knowledge and support. Look for programs with robust mentorship and access to a thriving traders' community.

5. In trading communities, diverse styles and strategies abound. Learn from others' experiences, receive support during tough times, and embrace collective knowledge for smarter decision-making in the dynamic market.

**Congratulations on finishing the book! Your dedication is appreciated. Now, could you spare a moment to share your thoughts in a review? Your insights can guide others. Thank you for being a part of our trading community.**

# Chapter 20

# Resources

## GLOSSARY

1. **Adapting to Market Changes:** The ability to adjust trading strategies and approaches based on evolving market conditions.

2. **Bear Market:** A market characterized by falling prices and pessimism among investors.

3. **Blue-Chip Stocks**: Shares of large, well-established companies with a history of stability and reliability.

4. **Bull Market**: A market characterized by rising prices and optimism among investors.

5. **Capital Gains**: Profits made from the sale of investments, subject to taxation.

6. **Cognitive Biases**: Systematic patterns of deviation

from norm or rationality in judgment, often influencing trading decisions.

7. **Combining Analytical Methods**: Blending fundamental, technical, and sentiment analysis for a comprehensive view of the market.

8. **Decision-Making Strategies**: Methods and approaches to make sound choices, especially in trading and investing.

9. **Diversification**: Spreading investments across different assets to manage risk.

10. **ETF (Exchange-Traded Fund)**: Investment funds traded on stock exchanges, mirroring the performance of a specific index.

11. **Financial Resilience**: The ability to withstand financial challenges and recover from losses.

12. **Flexibility in Plans**: Emphasized as crucial, flexible trading plans allow traders to adapt to market shifts, seize new opportunities, and shield themselves from risks, promoting long-term success.

13. **Fundamental Analysis**: Examining a company's financial health through income statements, balance sheets, and cash flow statements.

14. **Goals in Trading**: Positioned as guiding stars, goals serve as checkpoints providing direction and focus,

ensuring a structured approach to decision-making and navigation of financial markets.

15. **Hedging**: Protecting against potential losses by off-setting risks.

16. **Index Funds**: Investment funds that aim to replicate the performance of a specific market index.

17. **Indicators for Technical Analysis**: Tools such as moving averages and RSI used by technical analysts to understand market prices.

18. **Internal Data**: A part of the Daily Trading Strategy, addressing the psychological and emotional aspects of trading.

19. **Leverage**: Using borrowed capital to increase the potential return of an investment.

20. **Limit Order**: An order to buy or sell a security at a specific price or better.

21. **Liquidity**: The ease with which an asset can be bought or sold in the market without affecting its price.

22. **Long-Term Investing**: Holding onto investments for slow, steady growth, benefiting from compounding returns.

23. **Market Capitalization**: The total value of a compa-

ny's outstanding shares of stock, indicating its size in the market.

24. **Market Conditions**: Choosing favorable market conditions and stepping away during unfavorable times.

25. **Market Order**: An order to buy or sell a security at the current market price.

26. **Market Sentiments**: How understanding psychology helps read market sentiments.

27. **Mechanical Data**: A part of the Daily Trading Strategy, focusing on the practical aspects of trading.

28. **Mentorship**: A relationship where an experienced individual guides and supports someone less experienced.

29. **Mindfulness**: The practice of staying present, helping traders make rational decisions despite emotional extremes.

30. **Mindfulness Practices**: Staying in the moment during trades to avoid emotional reactions.

31. **Monthly Cap**: The maximum allowable risk in terms of financial capital in a single month.

32. **Options Trading**: Contracts that provide the right, but not the obligation, to buy or sell an asset at a

predetermined price.

33. **Portfolio Management**: The art of selecting and managing a collection of investments to meet specific financial goals.

34. **Preventing Impulsive Reactions**: Emotional discipline as a key to preventing impulsive reactions.

35. **Protocol**: A clear plan guiding trading decisions and maintaining organization.

36. **Real Trading**: The execution of trades using real money rather than in a simulated or practice environment.

37. **Recap of Key Strategies**: Let's quickly revisit the important strategies we've picked up.

38. **Resilience in Turbulent Markets**: The ability to stay strong amidst market fluctuations by accepting market ups and downs as normal.

39. **Review and Adjust Strategies**: A continuous improvement process involving the analysis of past trades for strategy refinement.

40. **Risk Adjustment Test (RAT)**: A crucial test to understand one's risk tolerance and trading style.

41. **Risk Appetite**: The level of risk an individual is comfortable taking on in their trading activities.

42. **Risk Assessment Test (RAT)**: A crucial test to understand one's risk tolerance and trading style.

43. **Risk Management**: Strategies to identify, assess, and prioritize risks while implementing techniques to mitigate or avoid them.

44. **Risk Management Plans**: Comparable to a battle strategy, these plans involve setting clear rules on money allocation, diversification, and regular reviews to safeguard capital and ensure overall portfolio health.

45. **Risk Management Rules**: Established guidelines to govern how traders' approach and handle risk in their activities.

46. **Risk Mitigation**: Strategies and actions taken to reduce the potential impact of adverse market movements.

# Chapter 21

# Annexures

## TRADING RESOURCES

Downloadable Resources (Just Click On The Given Links For Redirection To Download Page)

**TRADING JOURNAL TEMPLATE**

# RISK MANAGEMENT WORKSHEET (AUTOMATED EXCEL FILE)

## MINDFULNESS REPORT

# EMOTIONAL JOURNALING READYMADE TEM-PLATE (PRINT AND USE)